AN INTRODUCTIO

CAD

BRIAN MAYOCK

Hodder & Stoughton

LONDON SYDNEY AUCKLAND TORONTO

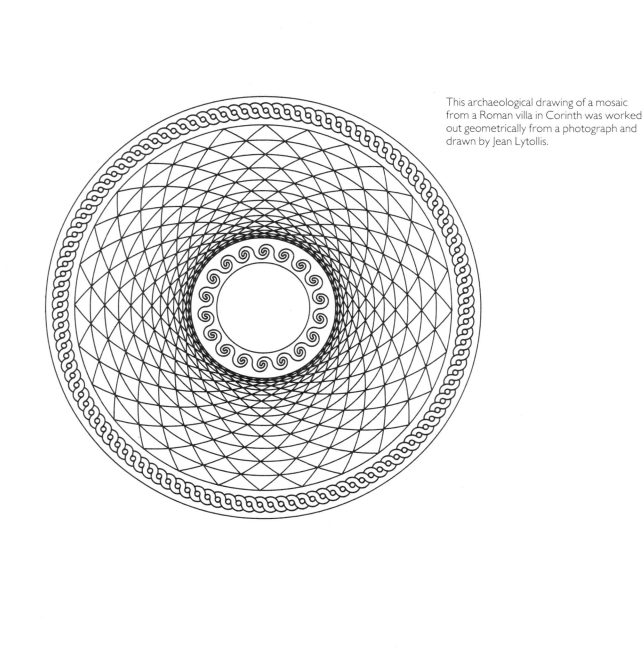

This archaeological drawing of a mosaic
from a Roman villa in Corinth was worked
out geometrically from a photograph and
drawn by Jean Lytollis.

British Library Cataloguing in Publication Data
Mayock, Brian
  An introduction to CAD
  1. Design. Application of computer systems
  I. Title
  745 . 40285

  ISBN 0 340 51969 X

First published 1990

Typeset by Litho Link Ltd, Welshpool, Powys.
Printed in Great Britain for the educational publishing division of Hodder and Stoughton
Ltd, Mill Road, Dunton Green, Sevenoaks, Kent by St Edmundsbury Press,
Bury St Edmunds, Suffolk.

CONTENTS

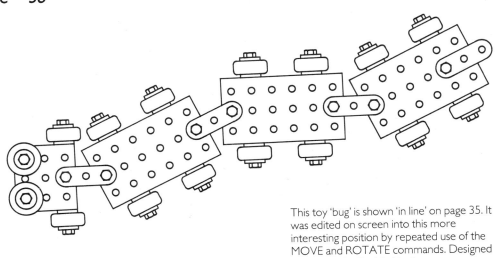

This toy 'bug' is shown 'in line' on page 35. It was edited on screen into this more interesting position by repeated use of the MOVE and ROTATE commands. Designed and drawn by Sophie Neal.

NOTES FOR TEACHERS

Designing

Fundamental to the process of designing is the skill of visualising how a part, shape or word will look in a variety of different ways or configurations. Drawings made by traditional methods are not easily manipulated since the process usually involves lengthy tracing and pasting-up. On the other hand, drawings made on a computer can be altered and rearranged quickly and easily until a satisfactory solution is achieved. It is this facility, together with the ease of retrieving stored information, which makes computer drawing such a powerful design tool. A designer still has to bring everything together in a communication for others to read. In this respect the *language of drawing* has not changed, and nor did it need to. The principles of geometry and projection remain the same and drawing practice, as internationally recommended, has been flexible enough to accommodate many new technologies. There has been no change in the way in which we 'read' drawings even if those lines are now drawn electronically on a screen. In fact, they end up as lines on paper in a *print-out*.

Aims

The intention of this book is to provide computer-aided drawing and design exercises which demonstrate the advantages of computer-aided drawing over traditional drawing-board based practice, especially in manipulating and storing shapes. The exercises are for use on any type of CAD software which incorporates an adequate range of drawing and editing facilities. It should be understood that CAD software is intended for use by people who know how to draw. At the present time, these drawing skills are best taught traditionally before starting CAD.

Skills

The assignments progressively incorporate new techniques with the first exercises directed towards *learning to drive a CAD package*. I hope the meaning of my mixed metaphor is clear, for without a good measure of practising the basic skills, little success in subsequent design assignments can be expected. In this respect, the National Curriculum for Design and Technology acknowledges the need to teach the skills which are needed for realising design goals (para 6 Terms of reference).

New skills which are being introduced are indicated along the bottom of each page for example, ● GRID ● SNAP ● LINE. The same method is used throughout the book to indicate the curriculum area associated with the assignment, demonstrating 'across the curriculum' opportunities; incidentally, showing that CAD has a versatility probably not envisaged by the software designers. Again, the National Curriculum emphasises the need for 'across the curriculum' activity in Design and Technology (para 1.8).

Software

In an effort to make them as universal as possible, these assignments have been worked on various brands of software, all of which do the same drawing tasks, more or less. Unfortunately, methods of working and terminology sometimes differ considerably (see table on page 12) and therefore detailed operating instructions covering all packages cannot be given. When more detailed information is needed manuals should be consulted. Some sequential instructions have been given, to assist the understanding of the initial assignments, based on two popular packages, *AutoCAD* and *Bitstik*. *AutoCAD* is the market leader in CAD worldwide and *Bitstik* is a well tried package based on BBC and Apple computers. Not all the available software has a full geometrical capability and this can seriously limit the range of work which can be attempted. In general, it has been my experience that cheap programs usually lack many essential functions; this can quickly lead to frustration and disenchantment with CAD systems. Fortunately, large educational discounts are generally available.

Presentation of information

In the initial assignments where sequences must be followed they are written in italics. Ordinary type indicates general information throughout the book.

Libraries of parts

Building up a library of frequently-used parts or symbols is an important part of the CAD technique. To gain full benefit, teachers will need to organise discs which can be used for this purpose.

Measuring by grid

Exercises are generally intended for working on a screen grid to save time in measuring and layout. Scales can be allocated to screen grids, and automatic dimensioning, which is becoming a feature of most software, also functions on grids. The use of screen grids links with the established use of grid or co-ordinate paper as a medium for design drawing. Preliminary planning on grid paper can be a considerable aid to thinking out ideas before starting on the computer.

Scope

The assignments in this book are limited to the type of work most 2D CAD packages are designed to produce. Isometric, oblique and planometric projections can all be drawn on snap grids which most CAD packages are capable of generating. Some software includes a 2.5D facility at present, but generally, genuine 3D software is in a price bracket which rules it out for schools at present. However, new developments are constantly being made and prices usually fall.

The National Curriculum

The National Curriculum has a thread of drawing and design activities running right through all levels. Computer-aided drawing begins at level 7. '*Pupils should be taught how to use computer-aided design and draughting techniques*' (p53). In reference to Information Technology the document states that '*IT is an essential component of Design and Technology*' (3.6 p73), and identifies one of the five aspects as, '*Pupils should be able to make effective and appropriate use of IT to capture, store, organise, access, modify, interpret and present information*' (3.5 p73). Assignments in this book, such as 24 Planometric Room Planning and 28 Design a Garden, will be a useful basis for developing teaching situations around such exemplars as, '*consider the use of a computer-aided design package to explore the ergonomics of kitchen design.*' (level 6 p77). An exemplar from

the interim document '*using graphic systems for creating drawings and patterns such as fabric designs*' (p67 interim) can be found in assignment 20 Pattern Design. An important point was made in the interim document which seems to have been overlooked in the final write-up. It rightly asserted that '*I T capability must be based on an understanding of principles and must avoid a clutter of detail which will soon become obsolete*' (p67 interim). Business software is already in general use which will take figures and turn them into instant graphs and charts. Such instant solutions, acceptable and necessary for commercial purposes, leave a lot to be desired in educational terms. Some of the underlying principles for presenting data and information are given with assignments, for example in assignments 32 Designing Graphs and Histograms and 33 Designing Bar Diagrams. The book as a whole has similar goals to those stated in paragraph 3.5. CAD software was designed to manipulate and store shape. It is clear that IT has a far wider brief than can be achieved exclusively through CAD software. However, CAD has to play a significant part.

Brian Mayock   *June 1990*

Acknowledgements

The author wishes to acknowledge the help and encouragement given by the Dean of the Faculty of Education and Design, Professor K J Rawson, MSc, RCNC, FRINA, FEng, FRSA, FCSD. Also the considerable assistance given by his colleagues John Worsley, Richard Thomas and especially Jean Lytollis for working most of the drawings in this book. His thanks are also due to Dr Gerry Gregory for checking the text; to Alan Harding and Annelise Miller of Richard Taunton College, Southampton for trying out material; and numerous teachers and students who have co-operated.

The author and publishers would like to thank the following for permission to use their photographs and material:

CalComp Ltd, p11; Austin Rover Group, p31; Fiat Auto (UK) Ltd, p31; Ford Motor Company Ltd, p31; Land Rover Ltd, p31; Vauxhall Motors Ltd, p31; Commonwealth Secretariat, Pall Mall, London, for the extract from The Commonwealth Factbook (1987), p59; BBC Enterprises Limited for the weather symbols, p60.

Techniques And Terms Used In CAD

Draw

CONTROL

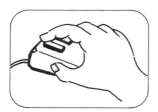

Moving a mouse, joy-stick, ball or pen controls the cursor on the screen. The button fixes the command.

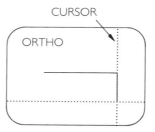

An XY cursor works like a tee-square and set-square. It keeps lines at right-angles.

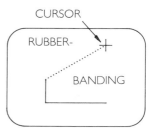

As the cursor is moved, a dotted line follows. This shows where the final line might be fixed.

Measuring & Co-ordinates

A computer screen is made up of thousands of tiny rectangles arranged in rows. These rectangles are called PIXELS. They turn on and off when instructed, producing lines or arcs of light. Each point on the screen can be found by measuring from the X and Y lines. 0,0 is usually at the lower, left corner of the screen.

● When drawing ABSOLUTE, all measurements are taken from the point of ORIGIN. See drawing right and above.

● When drawing RELATIVE, measurements are taken from the LAST measurement. Note that the start of a figure is best measured absolute.

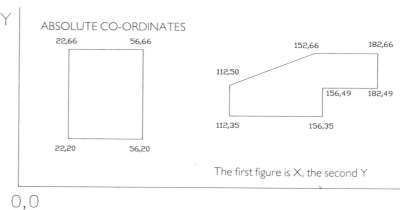

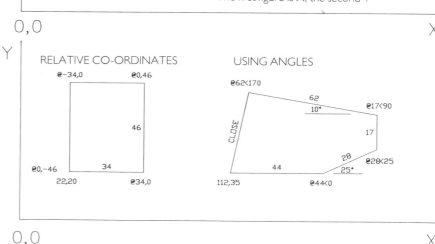

Grids

SQUARE GRID   ISOMETRIC GRID

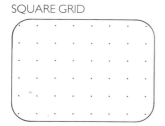

SNAP

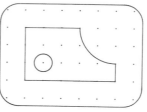

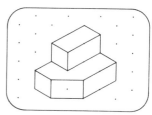

Very accurate grids can be set up on the screen. These are sometimes called snap grids because the cursor can only 'snap' to fixed points. Pictorial grids can also be set.

On some software, grid and snap mean the same. On other software, you can set snap to work at points between the grid. This is usually at half grid.

Linetypes

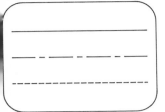

Some software will draw different types of lines.

Other software draws solid lines first and then alters them through CHANGE. Some software uses the plotter to change the linetype.

Offset

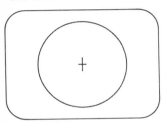

OFFSET will draw a line parallel to a selected line, arc or circle at a specified distance.

Circles

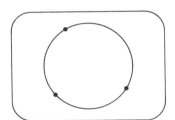

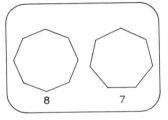

- Circles with given centre and radius or diameter are entered by keyboard or dragged to grid point.

- Three-point circles are drawn through any three points.

Polygon

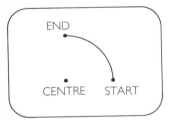

Drawn with a given length of side and number of sides or with a given number of sides and diameter.

Arcs

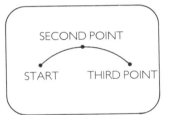

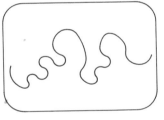

- Partial circles. This is a SCE (*Start, Centre, End*) arc, drawn anti-clockwise.

- Three-point arc. No centre is needed and arcs can be started in either direction.

Freehand

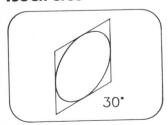

Free lines on CAD software use a lot of memory, so use sparingly. This does not apply to PAINT programs which use a different method of working.

Isocircles

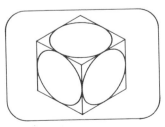

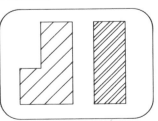

An isometric circle is an ellipse which fits into an isometric square.

ISOPLANES are the three surfaces of an isometric cube.

Hatch

Hatching lines will fill an area providing the outline is complete.

Limits

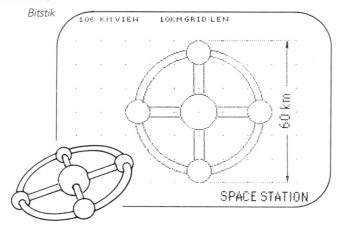

Scale

The screen is like having a sheet of paper on which you can draw (in *real sizes*) objects which vary from less then 1 mm to over a 1000 km. You set the screen by deciding the overall limits of the drawing. In the case of the space station, the drawing paper needs to be 100 km long. In the case of the watch bearing, the drawing paper needs to be 1 mm long. Given the overall size of the drawing required, *Bitsik* sets a suitable view and grid automatically. Other software may require the limits and grid to be selected. Having set the basic page, ZOOM is used to magnify different areas of the screen and any degree of detail can be added to the same scale.

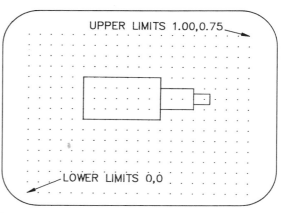

Screen setting for the Watch Bearing on *AutoCAD*

Zoom

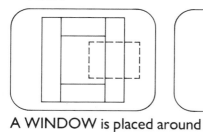 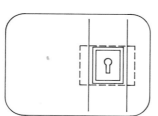 

A WINDOW is placed around the appropriate part of the drawing. This area is then enlarged to fill the screen.

You can add further detail by zooming again and again. If you reduce the drawing to original size, all of the detail is embedded.

Returning to the original size is called ZOOM ALL. See page 12 for variations.

Pan

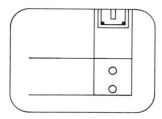 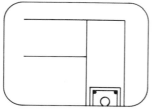

When in ZOOM, PAN brings adjacent parts of the drawing to the screen. It is like sliding the drawing paper about under the screen.

Default

Default values are basic settings. Changes can be made as needed during drawing. These are then shown within brackets as the most recent setting, e.g. Snap spacing <5>:
If this is the size you require just press RETURN.

Layers

LAYER 0

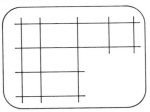

LAYER I

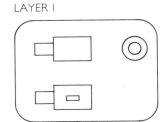

Layers allow work at different stages to be kept separate. A colour screen is necessary to show different layers.

Layer 0 layout
Layer I outlines
Layer 2 centre lines
Layer 3 dimensions

Mirror

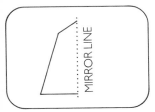 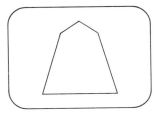

You need only draw half of the shape when the whole is symmetrical. The other half is mirrored. This function is sometimes referred to as a FLIP.

Move

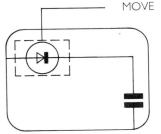 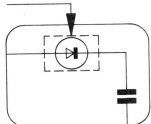

A unit or symbol can be picked up and moved to another place on the screen.

Erase

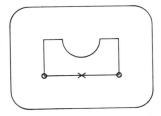 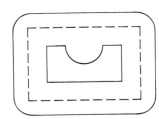

You can find and **mark** any line drawn on the screen and remove it by pressing return.

You can **window** whole areas and erase every line within the window.

Array polar

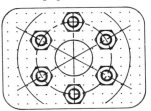

An array is a regular spacing of an entity in a circular or rectangular pattern. The number of items and the angle to fill must be entered. In this case there are 6 items in 360 degrees.

Array rectangular

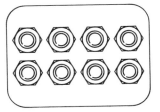

This is a rectangular array.

The number of rows and columns must be entered. In this case there are 2 rows and 4 columns.

Redraw

REDRAW will clean up the display by removing marks and blips which are the result of editing. Grid dots, which have been removed when erasing lines, will be replaced. If 'debris' remains after a redraw further erasing is needed.

Part Erase/Trim/Break

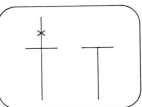

ERASE usually removes the whole line. TRIM and BREAK allow you to remove part of a line.

Fillet

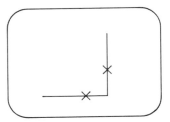

Some software will fillet corners given the radius.

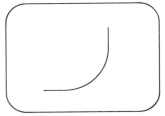

The radius will be blended and corner lines removed.

Line/Arc

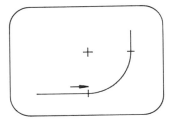

Tangent arcs can also be used to produce fillets providing the arc is drawn as the CONTINuation of a line.

Tangents

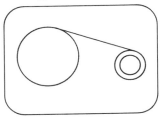

A box is placed on the circumferences near where the tangent is required. Exact points will be drawn.

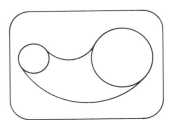

Curves can be blended in various ways. The top is by using FILLET. The bottom is by using TTR (*T*angent, *T*angent, *R*adius).

Text

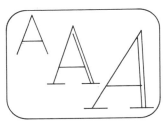

Notes on drawings, titles and instructions are typed in using TEXT. Sometimes a choice of style is offered in addition to various heights.

Find a point

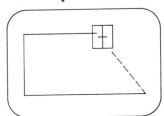

It is impossible to find the exact end of a line if it is not on a grid/ snap point.

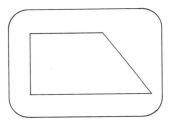

By placing a box around the end and using OSNAP the line will snap to the exact point.

Copy

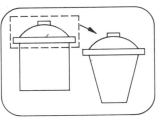

This function saves time redrawing the same thing. It is useful in designing to repeat one part and then add different shapes.

Parts file

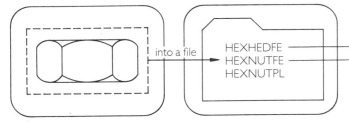

Commonly used parts can be drawn and saved to form libraries of parts which can be used again and again.

Insert

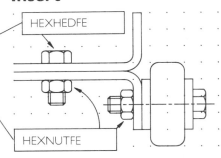

● When the block is brought out of file it is INSERTED into the new drawing.

Insert

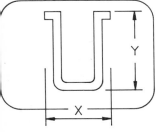 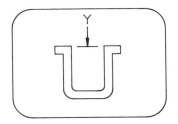

- When a block is inserted the shape can be changed vertically or horizontally by altering the proportions of the X and Y co-ordinates.

Rotate

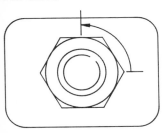 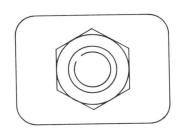

This nut has been rotated by 90°.

Save

SAVE will commit to file whatever is on screen at the time. You should **save work regularly**. A power cut can wipe everything that is not on file.

Quit

QUIT clears all work from the screen and returns to the main menu. Current work will be lost if not previously saved.

Plotters

 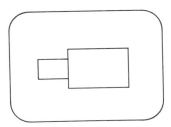

XY plotters take co-ordinates and convert them into lines on paper.

Scale, colour and linetype can be changed by using commands in the plotter software.

Stretch

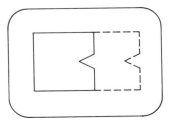

STRETCH is most useful for increasing one dimension of a shape.

Divide

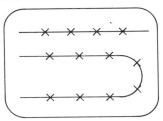

DIVIDE allows you to divide a line into a specified number of parts of equal lengths.

Dimensioning

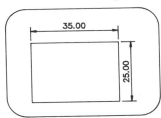

DIMENSIONING conventions can be set to operate when the line, angle, radius or diameter is selected.

Printers

highly magnified

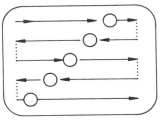

Dot matrix printers scan the screen line by line and print the pixels which are lit. This process is called a **screen dump**. Daisy wheel printers are unsuitable for technical drawings.

Table of Terminology

The following is a table showing some of the differences in terminology found in a selection of 2D CAD software. It was clear when researching the previous section that although software designers had written sequences which did similar drawing operations, a variety of names for these sequences had resulted from their individual efforts. These differences have made it difficult to write comprehensive instructions which apply to all packages; therefore, teachers will need to translate some of the terminology to the particular package in use. Unable to fall back on official standardisation, an arbitrary decision had to be made for this book, which was to use *AutoCAD* (which is acknowledged as one of the most comprehensive packages available) as the basis for the list of terms. The table has been compiled with the aid of user reference manuals, and apologies are made for any misinterpretation of manuals which might have occurred, or any alternative ways of working which might be possible. Software version numbers have not been given since up-dates do not usually change terminology. However, new operations may be added. For this reason, readers are advised to consult manuals supplied for more accurate information. The table was compiled to supplement the section on 'techniques and terms' and is in no way a comparison of the merits of the software included in the selection.

	AMX Design	AUTOCAD	AUTO-SKETCH	BITSTIK	COMPASS Starter	DRAW Mac	MICAD 2D	PAINT Mac	RM CAD	ROBOCAD	TECHSOFT
Rubber-banding	√	√	√	√	√	√	√	√	—	√	√
Co-ordinates	—	√	√	—	√	—	√	—	√	Delta mode	√
Square Grids	√	√	√	√	Guide	√	√	√	√	√	√
Isometric Grids	—	√	√	√	—	—	—	—	—	√	√
Snap	√	√	√	√	Lock	√	√	√	√	√	√
Isocircles	—	√	—	—	—	—	—	—	—	—	Ellipse in rhombus
Linetypes	√	Draw & use change	√	Change in plotter	Change in plotter	√	√	√	—	Select on menu	Change in plotter
Circles	√	√	√	√	Radius x 360°	√	√	√	Radius x 360°	√	√
Arcs	√	√	√	√	Radius x angle	√	√	—	Radius x angle	√	√
Blending arcs	—	√	—	—	—	—	—	—	—	√	√
Line/arc Continue	—	√	—	Tangent arcs	—	—	—	—	—	Tangent arcs	
Offset	—	√	—	—	—	—	—	—	—	—	—
Polygon	Rectangle triangle	√	√	—	—	Rectangle unequal	—	Rectangle unequal	—	—	—
Hatch	Fill	√	√	√	√	Fill	√	Fill	—	√	√
Freehand lines	—	Sketch	—	Trace	√	√	—	√	—	Stream	Sketch
Scale drawing	Rulers	Limits	Limits	View	√	Rulers	√	—	In plotter	√	√
Zoom	Zoom out	√	√	√	√	Enlarge	√	Fatbits	Zoom+	√	√
Zoom All	Zoom in	√	Zoom Limits	Page	Normal	Normal	ZI	Fatbits	Zoom−	Redraw	Zoom off
Pan	—	√	√	√	√	Scroll bars	—	—	—	√	√
Find a point	—	Osnap	Attach	Find	Hunt	—	—	—	Auto snap	Find	Hunt
Layers	√	√	√	—	—	Stacking	—	—	—	√	—
Array	—	√	√	—	Repeat + Rotate	—	—	—	—	Radial grids	Rotate
Mirror	—	√	√	Flip	Reflect	Flip	√	Brush mirrors	—	√	√
Move	—	√	√	√	Step Slide	√	√	—	—	√	√
Copy	—	√	√	√	—	Duplicate	—	Repeating copies	—	Duplicate	Repeat
Erase	√	√	√	√	Kill	Clear	Delete	Clear	√	√	Delete
Partial erase	—	Trim Break	Break	—	—	—	—	Eraser	—	√	√
Fillet	—	√	—	—	√	—	—	—	—	√	√
Tangents	—	√	—	—	—	—	—	—	—	√	√
Parts File	Macro	Blocks Wblocks	Catalogue	Visual library	U.D.C. library	Clipboard Scrapbook	—	Clipboard	—	Visual library	Data disc
Insert	Import	√	Part	Copy	Draw	Paste	—	Paste	—	√	Add
Stretch	—	√	√	√	—	Resize by drag	—	Resize by drag	—	√	√
Rotate	in 90°	√	√	√	√	in 90°	—	in 90°	—	√	√
Dimensioning	—	√	√	√	√	√	√	—	—	√	√
Text	√	√	√	√	√	√	√	√	—	√	√

PARTS FILE

In addition to the usual file of drawings, create a file of useful parts. The idea is to keep copies of standard drawings or part drawings in a separate file so that they can be found easily and used over and over again in new situations without the need to redraw. The facility to store and repeat is a major feature of computer-aided drawing.

File Names

Usually, file names must be created using no more than eight letters, without spaces or commas. It is not an easy task to make the meaning clear and easily recognisable (a) to others reading the list, or (b) when returning at a later stage to find a drawing. Suggestions are given for file names with each assignment.

On *AutoCAD* a small part of a drawing can be extracted, as a WBLOCK, for future use. Blocks can only be used on the same drawing. A WBLOCK can be used on other drawings. This stands for **write to file blocks**.

PARTS FILE

KNOB 2
CIRCLE 5
CIRCLE 6
PENTAGON
HEXAGON
PHILHEAD
HEXHEDPL
HEXHEDEE

Throughout the book these symbols mean:

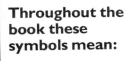

Save in PARTS FILE

PHILHEAD

File name of part to be inserted

INSERT

SAVE

AUTOCAD MULTI INSERT (MINSERT)

BITSTIK - COPY
ROBOCAD - INSERT

DRG FILE

WINDOW
HOUSE
HAIRDRYR
BALLJNT
DIMSWICH
GARBLK1

Robocom Bitstik and *Robocad* have visual filing systems. This illustration of *Bitstik* was made by copying the whole screen on to a printer. The process is called **making a screen dump**.

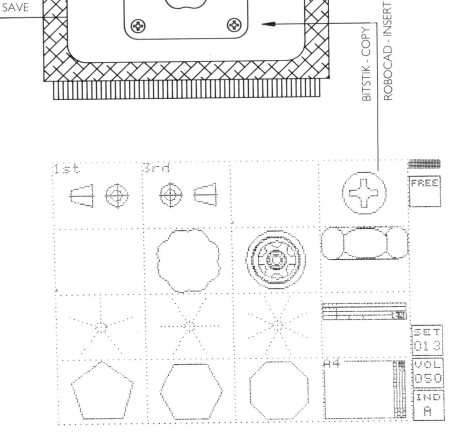

BORDERS & PROJECTION SYMBOLS

Title blocks and borders, once drawn and placed on file, save a considerable amount of repetitive drawing. They should be designed to satisfy the requirements of your school. The proportions for these symbols are taken from the British Standards Institution PP 7308, Engineering Drawing Practice for Schools and Colleges, 1986.

The symbols should be filed separately. They can be made more universal by incorporating them into the title block as shown. However, when reduced to very small proportions the centre lines may be confusing, so they should be removed before insertion.

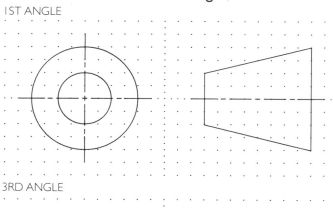

1ST ANGLE

3RD ANGLE

Parts File

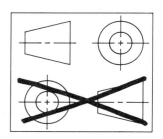

The grid size is not important, but the proportions of the views are. Count the squares carefully.

30

The 3 : 2 proportions of this border will fit 'A' size sheets of paper. Select a scale of plot to leave about 10 mm outside the border at the sides. Plant the border towards the bottom of the sheet of paper. This will give a wider portion at the top which will be useful for punching file holes.

Parts File

20

File name:
BORDER

Name		Title	
Date	Sheet of	School	

How to border a drawing

1

If the drawing is on screen SAVE the completed drawing.

QUIT will wipe the screen and return to the menu.

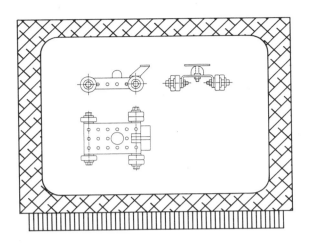

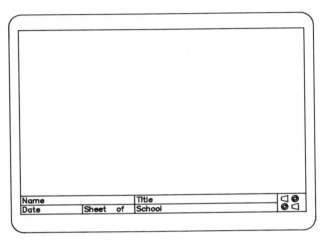

2

Bring the existing BORDER back to the screen.

If you are using your own disc it is worth having your name in the panel permanently. This can be done when you make the panel and border or it can be added and re-filed.

3

INSERT the drawing on to the screen. Reduce it to a suitable size and move it into an appropriate position.

Other drawings can be brought to the screen and composed to make a balanced communication.

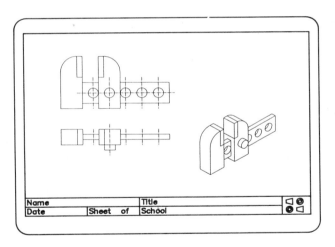

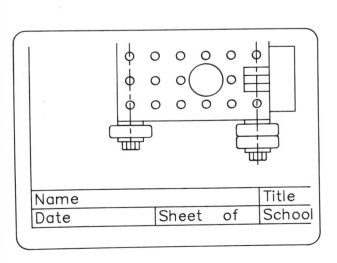

4

ZOOM and fill in details of name, title, etc., by using TEXT.

You may find it easier to align the text with the existing text in the panel by turning the GRID/SNAP off.

1
DRAW

Drawing these practical shapes will help you to find out what some of the drawing and editing commands will do. Working on screen is not difficult. If you make a mistake just UNDO or ERASE it and start again.

1 Begin on the MAIN MENU. Select 'begin NEW drawing'. Type in the file name PRINTER (see page 13). The default screen will appear.

2 Draw the outline. Select DRAW – LINE. All lines start and end on a grid/snap point. Count the squares for measurement.

*3 Start at any corner. Move the cursor on the screen from point to point. It will **rubber-band**. To draw the line press LH button on mouse. To stop drawing lines press RH button or RETURN on the keyboard.*

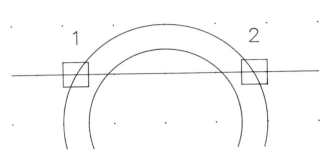

6 ZOOM up around the knob. Select TRIM or BREAK to remove the line between 1 and 2. Use INTERSECT to find the exact points 1 and 2.

7 SAVE the same file name. Then QUIT and you will be back to the main menu.

If your software is without **BREAK** or **TRIM**:

Zoom up for accuracy. Draw lines **on top** of the existing lines up to the circle. Take off the snap to meet the circle. Then erase the underneath line. Redraw or regenerate the screen.

Note: When two lines occupy the same space on the screen they cancel each other out and will disappear. When you redraw after erasing one line the other will reappear.

5 mm GRID/SNAP

ZOOM

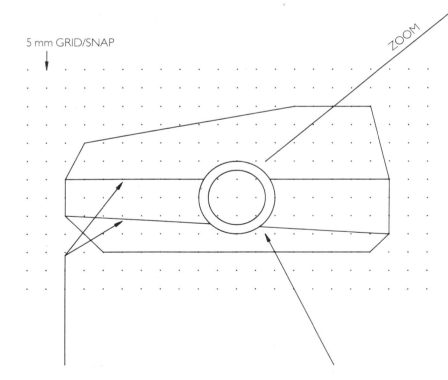

4 Draw these lines in full. They will be edited later.

5 Select DRAW – CIRCLE. Add the concentric circles 20 and 15 mm diameter.

File name:
KEY

GRID/SNAP 5 mm

1 Draw corners square then use FILLET. Radius 10 mm. Or use tangent arcs (see page 10).

2 This is a THREE-POINT ARC. No centre is needed.

3 To draw this fine detail change the SNAP to 2.5 mm.

File name:
GAME

This is a preliminary design for a game using ball-bearings which are propelled around a spiral groove. Getting balls into the various holes will score points.

If the software has an OFFSET command only draw the outer line and offset the inner line.

Use TRIM or BREAK

When drawing these ARCS you need to identify the START-CENTRE-END.

They can also be drawn as continuous tangent-arcs. In which case, start with a straight line.

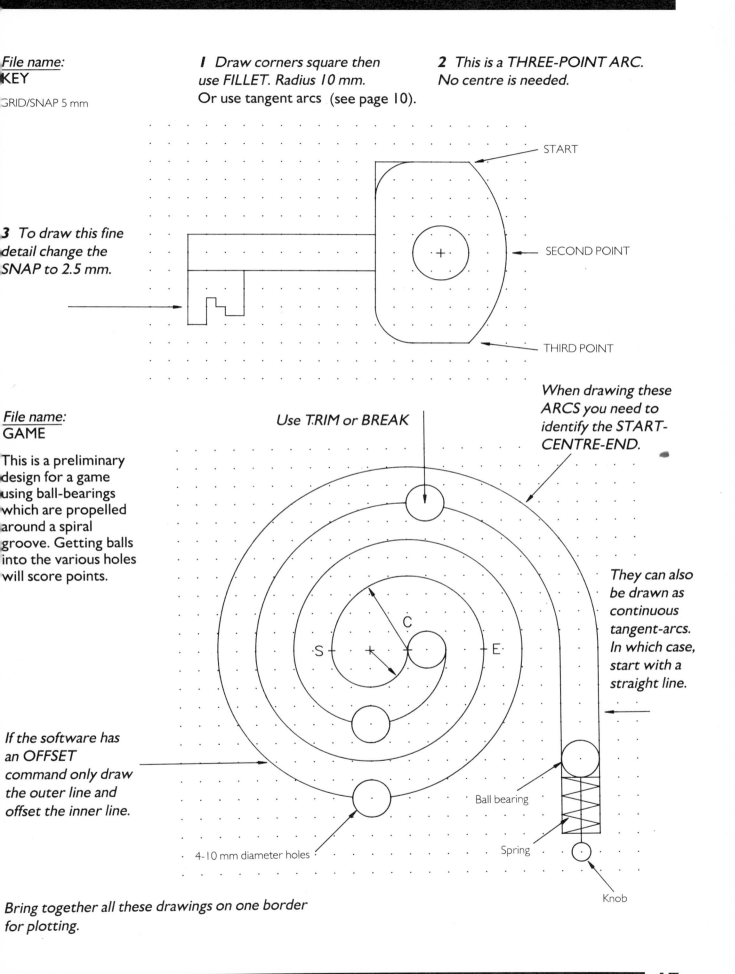

START

SECOND POINT

THIRD POINT

Ball bearing

Spring

Knob

4-10 mm diameter holes

Bring together all these drawings on one border for plotting.

2
HOUSE

Drawing a large object on a small screen

The elevation of the house is 7800 mm wide. A grid of 300 mm will work out at 26 squares for the elevation. The basic window will be 3 × 2 squares or 900 × 600 mm in real sizes. Allowing space at each side of the elevation, 9600 mm will be a suitable page size. Therefore, 9600 is the horizontal LIMIT. To fit the screen the vertical limit is always three-quarters of the horizontal. So, set LIMITS at 9600,7200 for this drawing. Note: Limits can be changed as drawing proceeds if you find more space is needed – but not if you run out of space on a drawing board.

This assignment will show you how CAD systems can be used to reduce the time taken to make complex drawings. The windows on file can be used over and over again and once on screen they can be moved about until the right design is obtained.

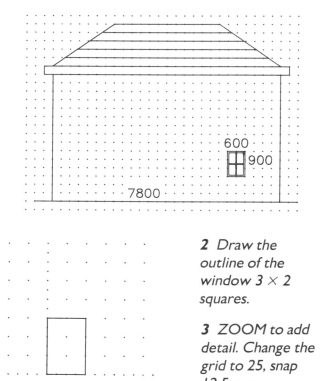

File name:
WINDOW

1 Start a new drawing using the file name.

On *Bitstik* start drawing centre screen. This is the only insertion point. When a drawing is redrawn from file on screen (INSERT), the insertion point is used to locate it exactly.

2 Draw the outline of the window 3 × 2 squares.

3 ZOOM to add detail. Change the grid to 25, snap 12.5 mm.

4 Use PAN to move the drawing up or down screen.

5 SAVE as WINDOW 1.

6 Edit the same drawing into a new design. SAVE as WINDOW 2. QUIT to clear screen.

Insertion point

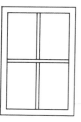
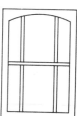

I Start a new drawing, using the file name.

2 Draw the house without windows or door.

3 Take lines through to next snap point and trim.

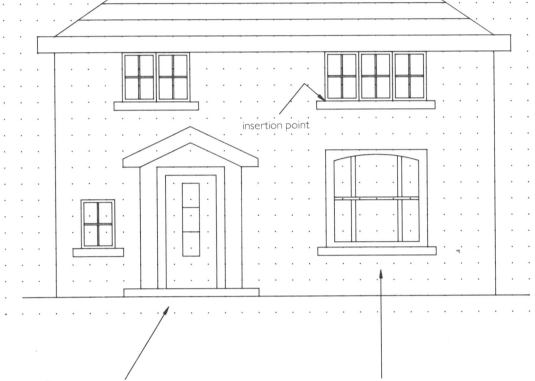

insertion point

4 SAVE. Do not quit.

5 Continue the same drawing. INSERT windows. Note where the insertion points will be. Use MOVE to change the design if required.

6 The entrance is for you to design.

7 All windows should be the same pattern throughout the house. When the drawing is complete SAVE as HOUSE 1.

8 Modifications, for a new design, can be made to the house and windows without the need to start again. The basic house is on file if needed.

File the new design as HOUSE 2. Note: The proportions of the window can be changed by altering the value of the Y scale factor when inserting.

Drawn on *MacDraw*

3
MONORAIL

File name:
-MONORAIL

This curve is a continuation of the previous line and is a tangent to it. Hence the name TANGENT ARC. Tangent arcs are useful for blending lines into arcs.

Start at A and draw a line to B. On Bitstik select TAN ARC and it will continue with an arc which will rubber band. Finish the arc at C. Other software may use a different name. For example, it is called CONTIN for a continuation arc on AutoCAD.

Detail of Wheel – Zoom

You can draw these radii by using a COMPASS ARC. Or, on software with a selective erase, draw the full circle and use BREAK to remove the unwanted parts.

When ZOOM is used, some software will keep the original grid setting. Others will need to be reset by halving the original spacing, which is in this case to 2.5 mm.

Mirroring

When a drawing or design is symmetrical you need to draw only half: the computer can be used to mirror the other half. This needs a little planning before you start. On *Bitstik* the drawing to be mirrored must be placed up to the centre of the screen. Other software will mirror around a line placed up to the drawing.

Set limits of 160, 120 or a 160 mm view
Grid 5 mm   Snap 2.5 mm

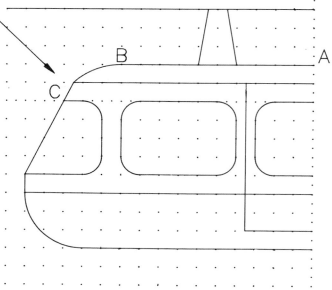

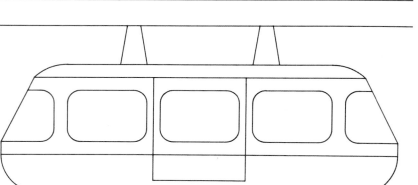

4
SUNGLASSES

File name:
SUNGLAS

Angles

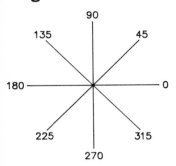

All angles, wherever they are placed on the screen, are drawn as if they had started from horizontal to the right (0 on the diagram) and increase in a counter-clockwise direction.

Each line is drawn RELATIVE to the last line. ABSOLUTE coordinates are measured from the bottom left corner. 0,0. (see page 6). The 'at' symbol – @ – starts the measurement from the last point recorded.

1 Using the grid, start in LINE at centre screen. Draw construction lines a and b.

2 Select LINE and place cursor at START. Turn GRID/ SNAP off. Type with a return at the end of each line –
@ 63 < 283
@ 58 < 7
@ 63 < 98
@ 62 < 193

3 FILLET the corners.

4 Complete the shape and MIRROR the other lens.

When shapes have many angles or curves a snap grid is of little help and can be confusing. This is such a drawing where it is easier to work without the grid. Lines are drawn by typing in the co-ordinates using the keyboard. The assignment could be difficult on software without a full range of facilities.

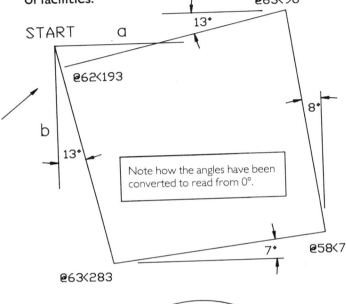

Note how the angles have been converted to read from 0°.

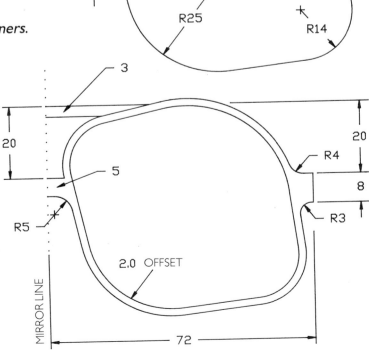

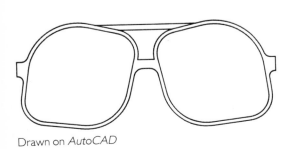

Drawn on *AutoCAD*

5
X y Flips

When the drawing has vertical and horizontal symmetry you only need to draw one-quarter of the pattern. The rest of the pattern can be mirrored. For an example of how this technique can be used in pattern design look at page 39.

Set limits of 160, 120 or a 160 mm view
Grid 5 mm   Snap 2.5 mm.

File name:
FLIPPAT1

Use this simple pattern to try out the mirroring technique. Your software manual will give more exact working details.

MIRROR LINE

MIRROR LINE

File name:
KNOB1

insertion point

File name:
FLIPPAT2

When the inner and outer radii have been drawn turn the grid off. If your software does not have INTERSECT snap, ZOOM up again for greater accuracy in finding the centres. Draw the ARCS and ERASE all other lines.

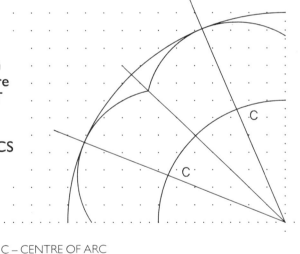

C

C

C – CENTRE OF ARC

File name:
KNOB2

insertion point

File name:
FLIPPAT3

These are useful shapes. They can be used as a basis for knob design and saved for future use.

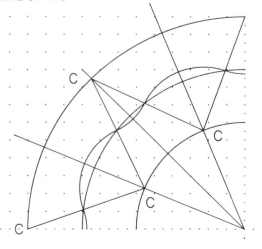

C

C

C

C

Parts
File

6
SCREWHEADS

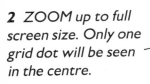
Parts File

This is a drawing for the parts file and it is needed for the hair dryer on the next page. The drawing will cover all crosshead patterns of screws such as Phillips and Posidrive. It is not necessary to draw more detail. It will only be lost when scaled down. The way you start and work depends upon which software you are using so two different examples are given.

AutoCAD 5 mm grid

On *AutoCAD* parts can be scaled up or down when they are inserted on screen. A convenient size to make a parts drawing is 1 mm. To scale the part up, multiply by the size required. A 10 mm head is multiplied by 10 and so on.

1 Start anywhere on screen. Draw a 1 mm diameter CIRCLE.

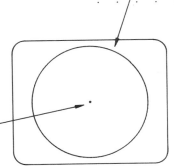

2 ZOOM up to full screen size. Only one grid dot will be seen in the centre.

3 Reset the GRID so that there are 16 grid spaces across the 1 mm diameter. 1 mm divided by 16 = 0.0625 mm.

4 Draw the shape of the head. Place the INSERTION POINT at the centre of the head. FILE.

5 The size of the INSERT is easily calculated. A 5 mm diameter head will be Scale Factor: 5 and so on.

Bitstik 5 mm grid

On *Bitstik*, part drawings in file cannot be inserted larger than the screen size originally drawn. Therefore, the technique is to start big and scale down to insert. Fixed ratios are 50%, 25% and 12.5%

1 Start centre screen. This is the only insertion point on Bitstik. *Make the diameter 8 grid spaces. (40 mm).*

2 ZOOM so that the diameter has 16 grid spaces.

3 Draw the shape of the head. Tangent arcs can be used to draw the fillets. FILE.

4 The 40 mm drawing will give scaled inserts of 20, 10 and 5 mm. So, the 5 mm diameter head, used on the Hair-dryer page 24, is an insert at 12.5%.

File name:
PHILHEAD

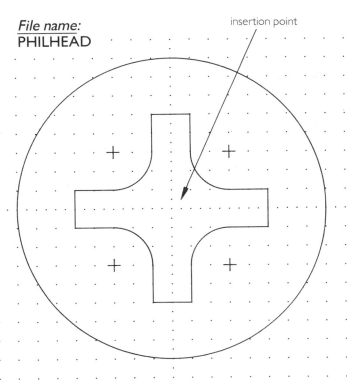

insertion point

File name:
SLOTHEAD

Draw a screwdriver slot head for the file. Make it the same size as the crosshead pattern. Place the slot at 45°. This avoids confusion with centre lines.

Draw a diagonal and OFFSET 5 mm at each side

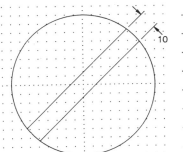

10

7
HAIR-DRYER

This assignment combines many CAD techniques. You will need to use ZOOM to draw the fine detail. Look for opportunities to apply COPY and MIRROR. These techniques save drawing time.

File name:
HAIRDRYR

Set limits of 320, 240 or a 320 mm view
Grid 10 mm   Snap 5 mm

Centre lines

AutoCAD — draw as continuous lines and use CHANGE.

Bitstik — Select a dotted line and change it on the plotter.

Robocad — Select centre line direct from the menu.

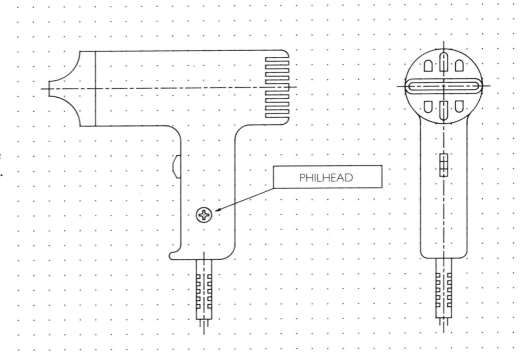

PHILHEAD

These details of the hair-dryer are zoomed up. You will need to reset the grid and snap to 5 and 2.5.

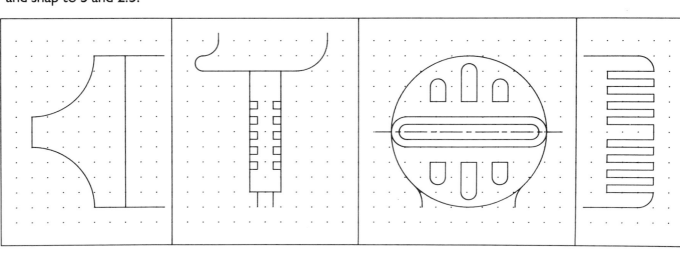

8 ISOMETRIC PROJECTION

File name:
PLUGS

When you are working on a drawing board you can produce isometric projections by drawing all the horizontal lines with a 30° set-square as shown below. On CAD grids the horizontal X rows can be rotated to 30°, and the vertical Y rows left at 90° to produce an isometric grid. Some software gives an automatic **iso-grid** command.

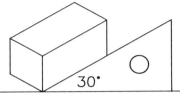

These drawings of electrical plugs have been simplified so that you need to use only straight lines.

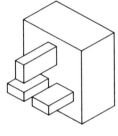

9 ISOMETRIC CIRCLES

File name:
ISOCIRCL

When you draw a circle in isometric projection it becomes an ellipse. If your software will not draw isometric ellipses they can be drawn approximately by using four arcs. These are continuous arcs running at a tangent to each other. This is why they are called **tangent-arcs**.

1 Set an isometric grid and mark out an isometric square.

2 On software such as Bitstik move the cursor from A to B to make a blind vector. Set the tangent-arc. Draw BC and continue through D and E back to B. AutoCAD calls this a line/arc situation.

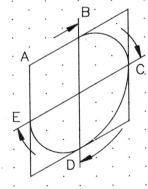

3 Erase the isometric square.

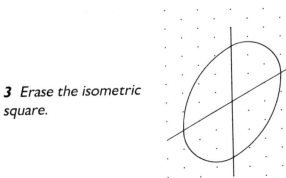

Draw an isometric circle in the horizontal plane. Start at a corner and draw a line to start the arcs.

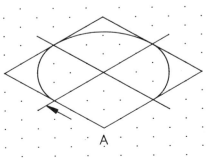

10
BALL JOINT

File name:
BALLJNT

This plastic ball joint was designed for constructing rectangular space-frames. You simply push plastic tubes of various lengths into the holes. Cover the sides with plastic sheet or net and they can be used in agriculture for greenhouses or fruit cages. The joint can be made in many different sizes. Can you think of other uses? Sketch your suggestions.

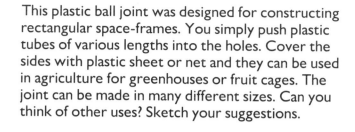

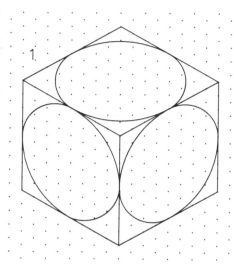

1 Draw an isometric cube with isometric circles.

2 Complete the circle by adding the three tangent-arcs.

3 Erase the cube.

This drawing shows the difference between an ellipse made with a true ellipse facility and one constructed with tangent-arcs.

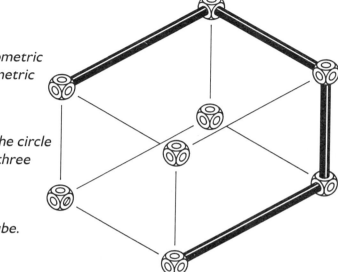

four tangent-arc ellipse

true ellipse

This drawing shows the ball joint drawn with true ellipses.

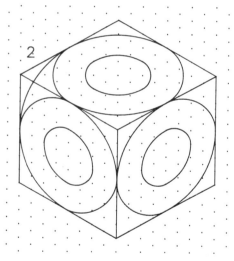

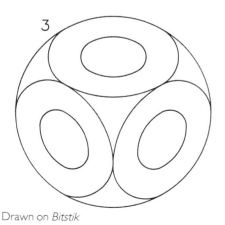

Drawn on *Bitstik*

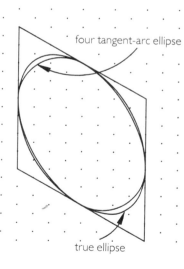

Drawn on *AutoCAD*

From the comparison you can see that the two methods do not match exactly. Because of this, it is best not to mix the constructions on the same drawing.

11

File name:
ADSCREW

Adjusting Screw

A screw thread is a helix. A screw like this can be seen on a vice in the workshop. Technical illustrators produce effective looking threads by drawing part ellipses. We can use the same method in CAD.

1 Draw the two isometric ellipses one grid space apart.

2 Erase all but the back thread up to the overlap intersection of the threads. File it so that it can be copied and repeated.

3 Lay out the box construction for the whole part. Plant the single thread along the centre-line. Erase the construction lines.

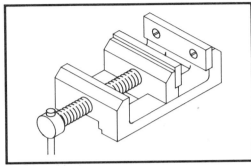

machine table vice

1

When using software without a part erase: Draw the two ellipses. Zoom up and draw the part thread on top of the rear ellipse. Erase the previous construction.

2

3

Location point. This must be centre screen on *Bitstik*. I have drawn these cross-lines only to show where to place the location point. Do not draw or file these lines.

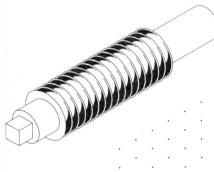

Highlights can make the thread look even more realistic.

Drawn on *AutoCAD*

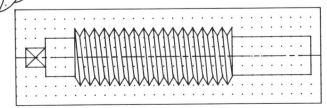

12
DESIGNING PEN TOPS

File name:
PENTOPS

Here are two designs for tops

The first design needs a feature to be added which will show the colour of the ink.

Safety

Young children have died after swallowing pen tops. They get stuck and stop air getting to the lungs. Redesign the tops to prevent this happening.

Sketch out ideas on grid paper and make plotted drawings of your final design.

Drawing cylindrical objects on software without isometric ellipses or trim

1 Construct a box which will contain the cylinder. Add all centre lines and diagonals.

2 The top can be drawn by starting with a line then changing to tangent-arcs for the curves.

3 The bottom is a half ellipse. Draw the full arc to the nearest grid point. Zoom up for greater accuracy and use the full arc as a guide for drawing the part arc. Then erase the full arc (see note on page 16).

The main function of a pen top is to seal the top of the pen to stop the ink drying out. A top can also be used to clip the pen in a pocket or bag. This part of the design relies on the plastic material having a small amount of 'give'.

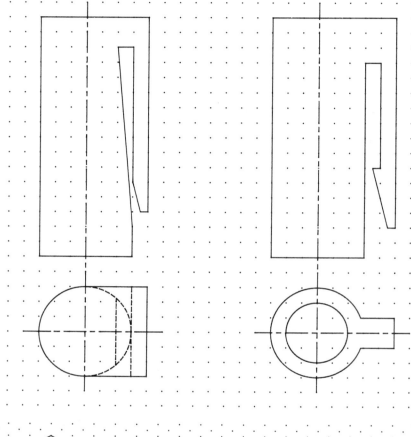

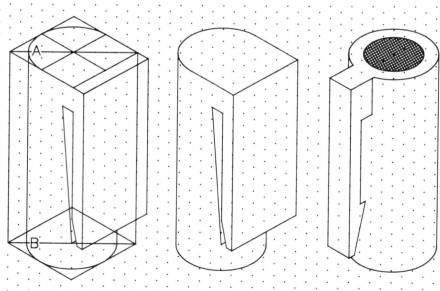

4 Move the grid to the end of the part arcs at A and B. Draw the vertical edges of the cylinder.

13
POLAR DIVISION

Parts File

When using software without a POLYGON or a POLAR DIVISION facility, it is worth putting these angular divisions and polygons on file. They will save considerable effort when working on later projects. Other divisions may also be useful to store.

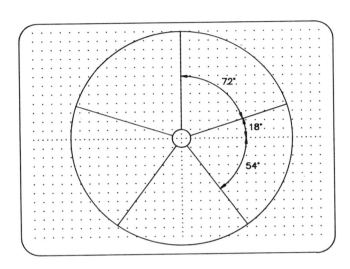

On *Bitstik* when a part drawing is inserted from file, the only point which can be used for accurate location is the centre of the original drawing screen. Many intersecting lines obscure the centre. A ring at the centre allows a clear view for locating.

1 Start at centre screen. Draw the 10 mm and 120 mm diameter circles. Mark out the angles up to the outer circle. The radial lines start at the centre.

File name:
CIRCLE5

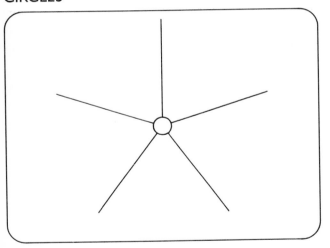

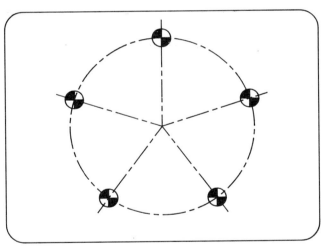

2 Erase the outer circle. File as CIRCLE5.

3 In use, CIRCLE5 can be inserted at any point on the screen. Any size circle can be drawn on it and five points located. Erase CIRCLE5.

File name:
CIRCLE6

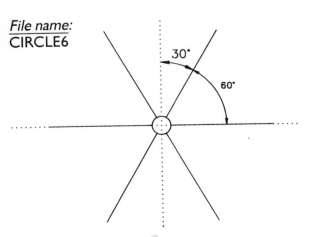

File name:
CIRCLE8

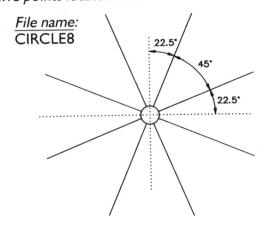

14 POLYGONS

This assignment uses the same angular divisions and polygons that appear in Assignment 13. Again, when using software without a POLYGON or a POLAR DIVISION facility, it is worth putting these parts on file.

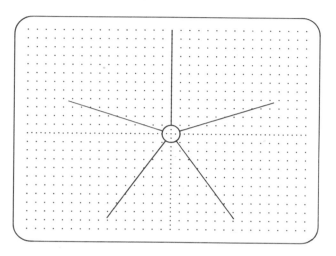

1 Copy CIRCLE5 and place centre screen at 100%.

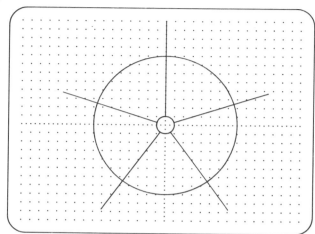

2 The circumscribing circle can be any size. Draw a large PENTAGON for the file.

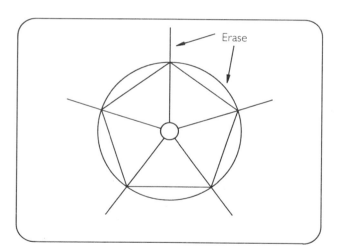

3 Turn the grid and snap off. Draw the sides of the pentagon. When an intersection snap is not available, ZOOM for greater accuracy. Erase construction lines and file as PENTAGON.

File name:
PENTAGON

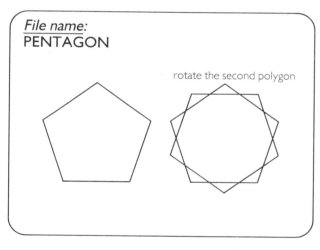

rotate the second polygon

4 These patterns were made by rotating a second polygon on top of the first.

File name:
HEXAGON

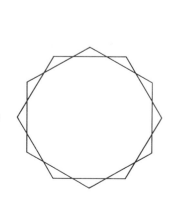

File name:
OCTAGON

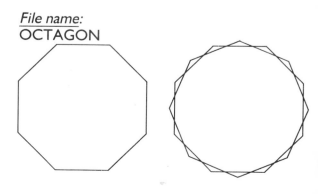

15
CAR WHEEL DESIGN

Car designers use wheel patterns to identify their makes. When many models in a range are very similiar the wheel designs become the most distinctive feature to look for. Note that all the designs are based on geometrical divisions of a circle. For example, the Vauxhall wheel is divided into five. What divisions are used for the other designs.

VAUXHALL

FORD

FORD

RANGE ROVER

FIAT

ROVER

This well known design has a distinctive logo in the centre. Can you discover the make of car? What image has been built up over the years by the design of this car.

Drawn on *Bitstik* by Tony Osgood

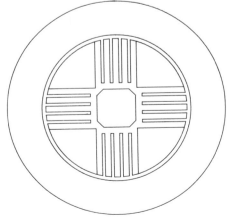

Car wheel designing

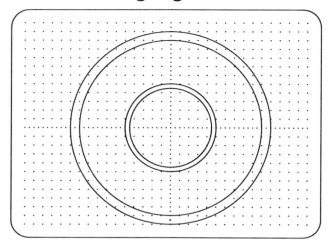

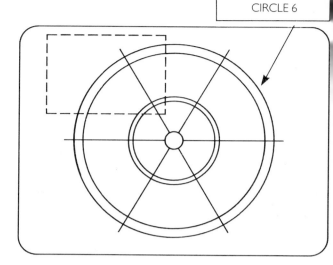

1 *Start at centre screen. Draw the 110, 100, 50, 45 mm diameter circles.*

2 *INSERT CIRCLE6 at centre screen. ZOOM to the area shown. Turn GRID off.*

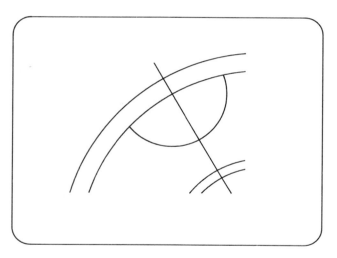

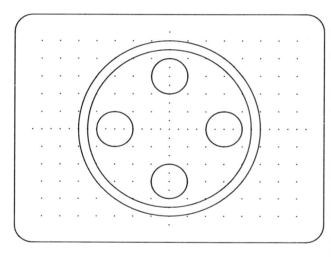

3 *Draw a 15 mm radius. If INTERSECT is available use it to find the centre. Repeat at six other intersections. The radius could be ARRAYED if available. ERASE CIRCLE6.*

4 *PAN to centre screen. Turn GRID ON. Draw the four 10 mm diameter circles. ZOOM ALL (PAGE) so that the whole drawing is displayed.*

This is the final result and a further example is given for you to work out and draw.

Sketch out other ideas for wheel designs before developing them on the screen. Plot all designs on one drawing.

File name:
CARWEEL1

File name:
CARWEEL2

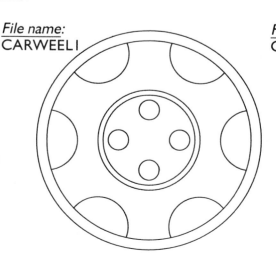

16
HEXAGON SCREW
HEADS & NUTS

Screws and nuts are designated by their diameter. These are views of a head and nut to fit an M20 screw. The M means metric. The proportions are based on British Standards PD 7300 with small modifications to simplify them for use on grids and for easier plotting. On *Bitstik* start at centre screen so that the centre mark can be used for insertion.

Hexagon head – Front elevation

File name:
HEXHEDFE

ZOOM and use 3 point arcs for all radii.

Hexagon head – Plan

File name:
HEXHEDPL

Hexagon head – End elevation

File name:
HEXHEDEE

Hexagon nut – Front elevation

File name:
HEXNUTFE

Hexagon nut – Plan

File name:
HEXNUTPL

The thread symbol is shown with the screw in place. This will be the most frequently-used case

Hexagon nut – End elevation

File name:
HEXNUTEE

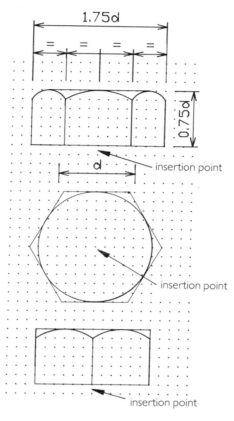

1.75d

0.75d

d

insertion point

insertion point

insertion point

insertion point

insertion point

insertion point

Set a 160 mm view or limits of 160, 120
Grid 2.5 mm   Snap 1.25 mm

METRIC SCREWS
DIA in mm
M 1.6
M 2.0
M 2.5
M 3.0
M 4.0
M 5.0
M 6.0
M 8.0
M10.0
M12.0
M16.0
M20.0
M24.0

1/8
1/4
1/2
1

Bitstick is locked to these fractions when inserting copy on default grids.

On *Bitstik* software copy can be inserted at ½, ¼ or ⅛ of full size. Thus, a 20 mm diameter drawing will reduce to give 10 mm, 5 mm, and 2.5 mm diameter drawings. Therefore, filing three sizes will cover most of the range — M24, M20, M16.

On software which can be scaled up, make the base drawing 1 mm diameter. Multiply by the size of screw when inserting.

Centre lines should be added after drawings have been planted.

17
SCREW & NUT

File name:
SCRW&NUT

You can now make a complete drawing of a screw and nut using the parts on file. The only parts to be drawn are the lines which represent the thread and the centre lines. These are things which will vary with each drawing. Make the thread 1/8 of the diameter of the screw. You should plant the nut on the screen before the thread is drawn.

Set limits of 160, 120
or 160 mm view
Grid 5 mm
Snap 2.5mm

HEXNUTFE

HEXNUTPL

HEXHEDFE

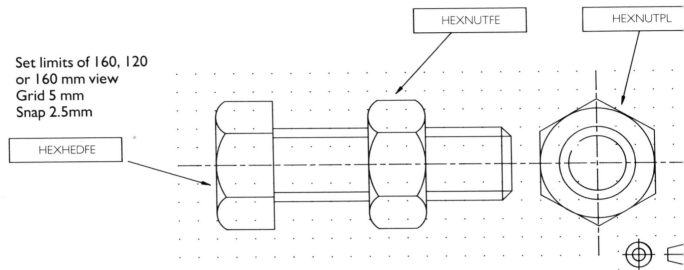

18
CONSTRUCTION TOY

File name:
CONSTOY

Develop a toy construction kit based upon the par[ts] shown below. Plastic screws and nuts will be used to fasten the parts together. Design the new parts and show an example of the type of model which could be built by using the kit. Put your initial idea[s] on to 5 mm squared paper. Material: plastic.

Develop this wheel assembly into a toy or a model by adding more parts, or make a completely new design of your own. Keep your designs simple. Children playing with the toy will use their imagination to fill in the detail.

If you are working on software which will not break or trim lines, ignore the problems which occur when parts of your design overlap.

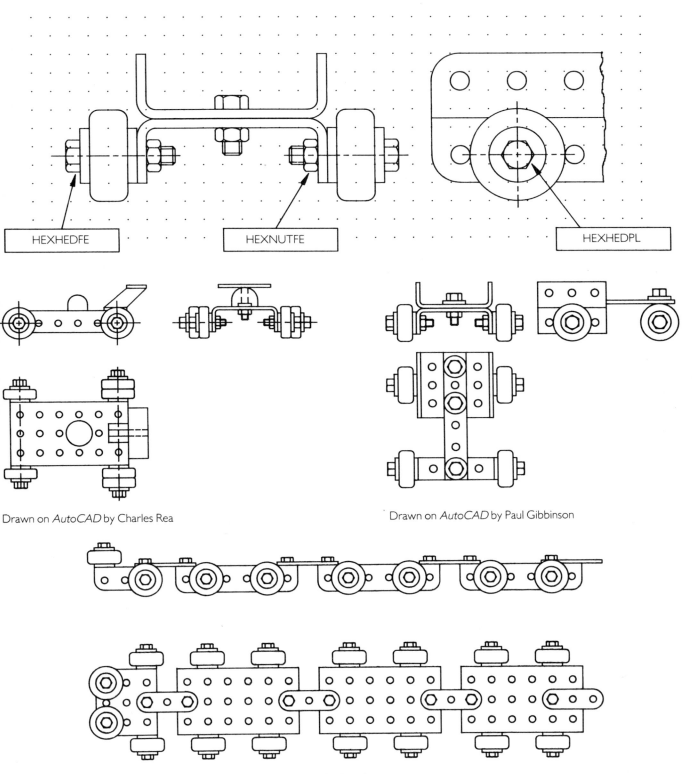

HEXHEDFE

HEXNUTFE

HEXHEDPL

Drawn on *AutoCAD* by Charles Rea

Drawn on *AutoCAD* by Paul Gibbinson

Drawn on *AutoCAD* by Sophie Neal

19 GEOMETRIC SCULPTURE

File name:
SCULP1

The aim of this exercise is to produce interesting sculptural forms based on joining together simple geometrical solids. The accuracy of X—Y plotters makes developments produced by CAD systems superior to those drawn traditionally. This is the development of a cube with circular holes cut out of the sides.

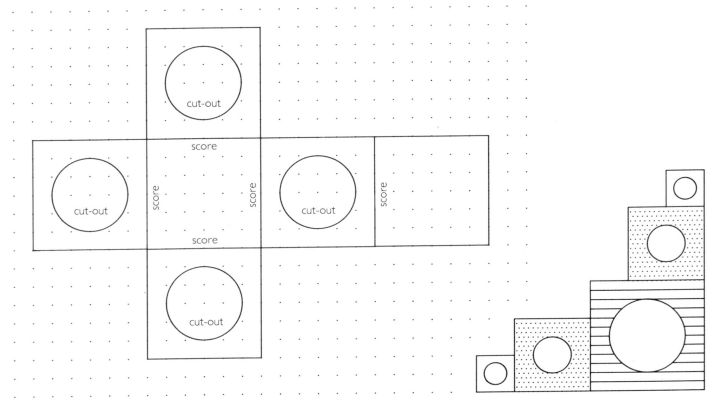

Plotting
Plot the cubes in three or four different sizes on thin card.

Cutting and gluing
Cut out using a sharp knife and safety rule on a piece of thick card or a cutting board. Score all bends. Glue edge to edge using a quick setting model glue.

Assembly
Start with the smallest cube and mount it inside the next size cube. Continue so that on completion each cube reveals that it has smaller cubes inside. Mount on a thick card base.

Painting
Paint with thick matt paint choosing colours to emphasise the different sides.

Experiment with other arrangements of the cubes which might make interesting geometrical sculptures.

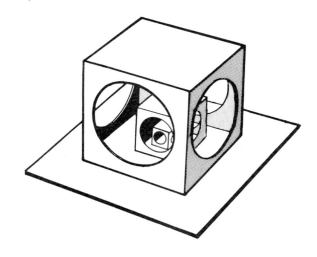

Surface developments based on equilateral triangles can be accurately plotted by using an isometric grid.

Always score lines on card before folding. Painting individual surfaces must be done with great care. Remnants of car spray paint can give a very effective finish but do it outdoors on a calm day!

Try joining together different solids to make pleasing forms.

Tetrahedron

File name:
TETRAHDN

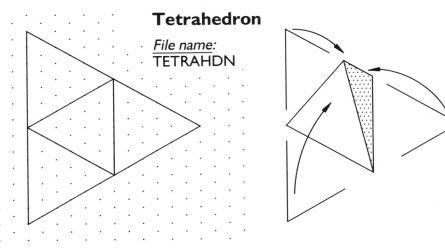

Octahedron

File name:
OCTAHDN

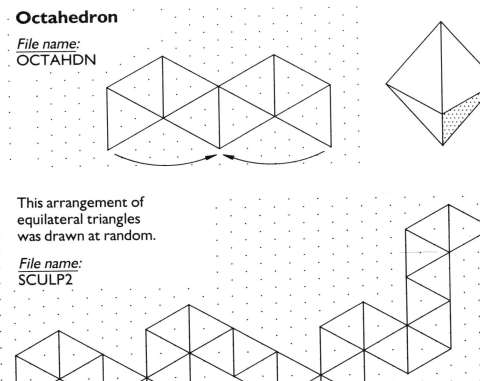

This arrangement of equilateral triangles was drawn at random.

File name:
SCULP2

These equilateral surfaces form cups and pyramids which can be painted in attractive colours.

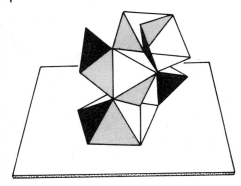

In mathematics, a surface development is described as a net or a tesselation. Look for more information about these five regular polyhedra: tetrahedron, hexahedron (cube), octahedron, dodecahedron and icosahedron. Four regular polyhedra developments can be drawn on square or isometric grids.

Which development cannot be drawn using these grids?

20
PATTERN DESIGN

Natural shapes such as leaves can provide inspiration for pattern design.

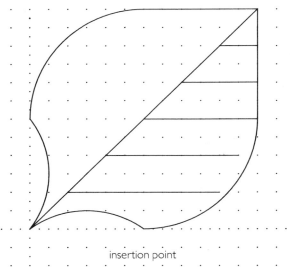

Convert the original shape into simple lines and curves.

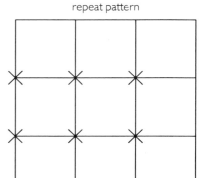

Silver birch leaf

insertion point

File name:
PATTDES1

repeat pattern

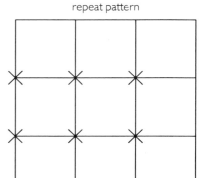

✕ insertion point

The leaf patterns shown below were inserted one pattern at a time. If an ARRAY command is available the same result can be obtained in one operation.

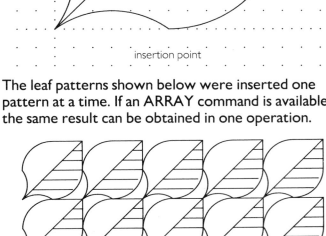

File name:
PATTDES2

half-drop pattern

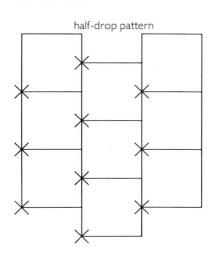

Drawn on *Bitstik*

File name:
PATTDES3

X and Y flips

You can create a highly complex design on computer drawing systems by mirroring and repeating basic patterns.

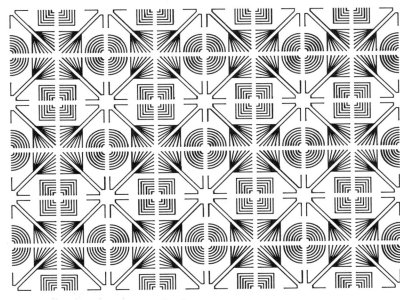

Drawn by Richard Sheppard, on *Bitstik*

Circular patterns

Circular patterns can be made by rotating polygons (see page 30). More complicated patterns need a POLAR ARRAY. The basic pattern should fit a division of 360°. For example, this paper plate pattern is 360° ÷ 12 = 30°. All construction lines must be erased before the pattern is arrayed around the centre.

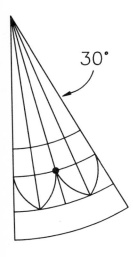

30°

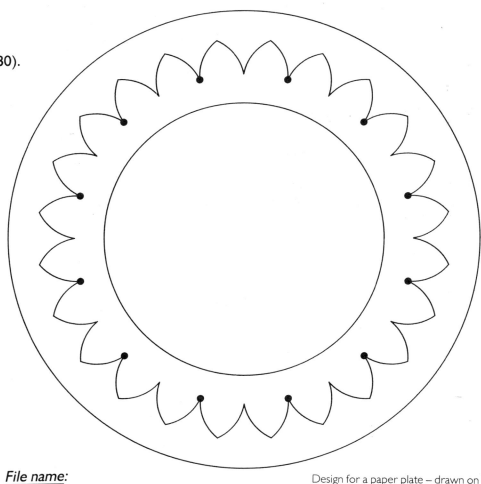

Design for a paper plate – drawn on *AutoCAD* by Jean Lytollis

File name:
CIRPATT1

21
TELEPHONE

You can develop an oblique projection from a front elevation by adding a side and top at 45°. The actual depth is halved to compensate for foreshortening due to perspective.

File name:
OBLICUBE

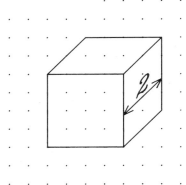

Draw the 4 × 4 × 4 cube. Depths are measured on the grid using the diagonals as units. They are halved.

File name:
KEYBOARD

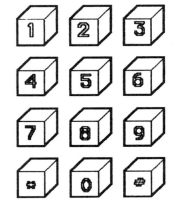

This cube can be used to draw a telephone keyboard by reducing and then duplicating it twelve times. Numbers should be placed on the keys after the reduction.

Make the keyboard part of a design for a one-piece telephone.

File name:
TELEPHNE

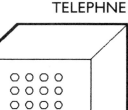

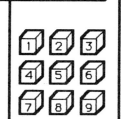

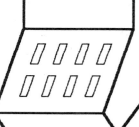

Drawn on *MacDraw*

22
SOCKET BAR

Oblique projection is a useful projection for drawing circular objects such as this bar. If the object is drawn with the circular parts facing front, they can be true circles. In isometric projection they have to be ellipses.

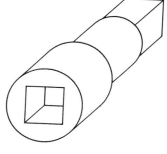

Drawn on *Techsoft Designer*

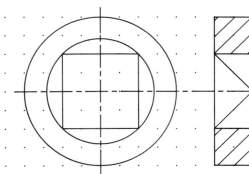

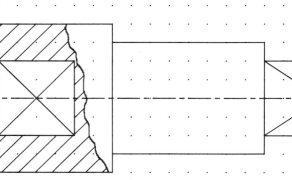

23 TOPOLOGICAL MAPS

File name:
MAPEWS

(England Wales Scotland)

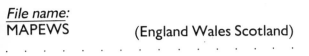

Topographical maps follow the outline of the coast as closely as possible. Tracing a detailed outline on to the screen uses up a lot of memory. A topological map, drawn only from horizontal and vertical lines, uses much less memory.

Designing a topological map

You will need to ask a teacher to help make an overhead projection transparency of a 5 mm grid. Place it over the ordinary map and tape it in position. Use a projection pen which will allow you to make corrections and convert the outline into a series of horizontal or vertical lines. Look at the overall shape and adjust it to make better sense where necessary.

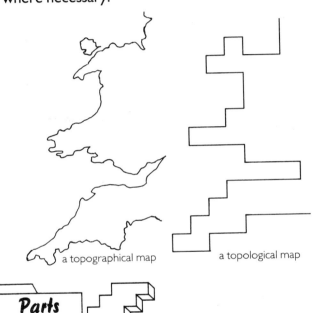

a topographical map   a topological map

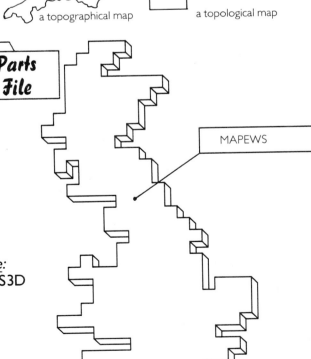

File name:
MAPEWS3D

A Three-Dimensional Map

Bring MAPEWS out of file and change the grid to half the original spacing. Add the oblique depth to the map.

24 PLANOMETRIC ROOM PLANNING

PLANOMETRIC is an oblique projection drawn to give a view looking down from above the object. You should choose to draw in planometric when the situation requires a 'true' view from above. Architects use planometric for room settings to show layout with a pictorial effect.

This is a good example of when to use planometric. Notice how the tiles on the top can be shown square and the circles do not need to be drawn as ellipses.

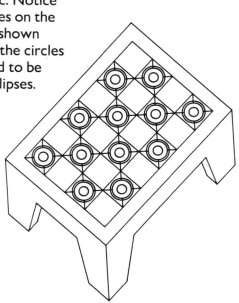

Planometric can be drawn on any square grid. Draw from diagonal to diagonal for horizontal lines and use the normal grid for verticals. This method can be used to foreshorten the vertical height.

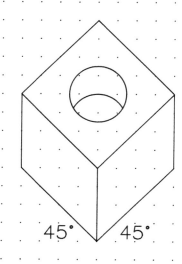

45°　　45°

You can improve these very basic drawings by zooming and adding more detail or by changing the shape of the furniture to your own design.

These are the basic outlines of living room furniture. Draw and file as blocks with individual file names, of up to eight letters. Use the bottom corner as insertion point. (This means starting at the centre on *Bitstik.*) Use the centre of circular objects.

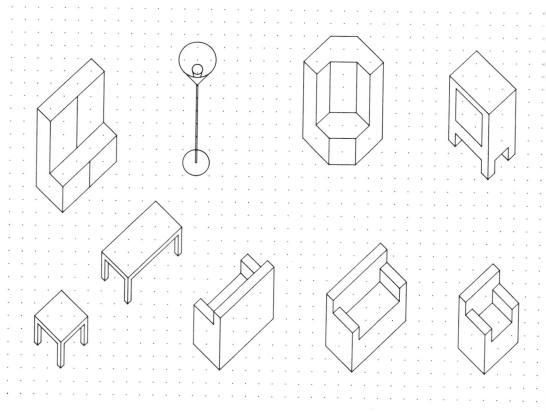

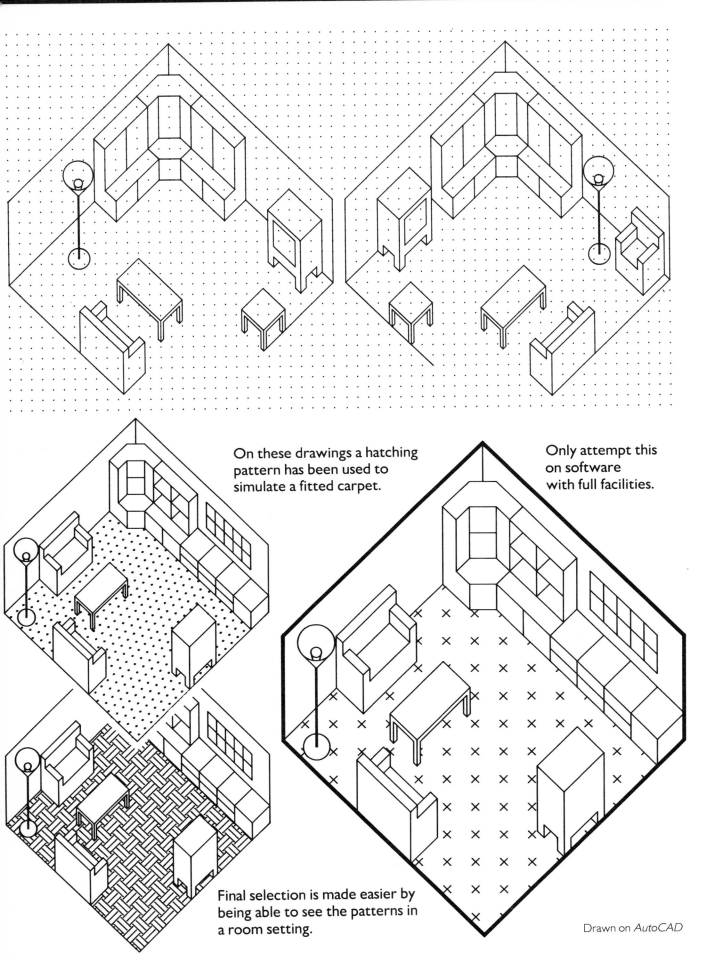

On these drawings a hatching pattern has been used to simulate a fitted carpet.

Only attempt this on software with full facilities.

Final selection is made easier by being able to see the patterns in a room setting.

Drawn on *AutoCAD*

25
GARDEN WALLING BLOCK

Make some preliminary drawings on squared paper using a ruler and compasses. Keep to straight lines and arcs. Draw one-quarter of the design, the try it on the screen. Mirror the three remaining quarters. Remember that the concrete must hold together around the shapes, so look carefully at what will be concrete and what will be holes through the block. Put the block on file so that it can be used to copy from. You will need an insertion point, or, if you are using *Bitstik*, file it up to the centre of the screen.

The wall shown on the drawing at the bottom of this page was made in three portions by first filing a section of sixteen block (i.e. 4 × 4), so that they could be inserted as one entry. Make a similar drawing based on your own design.

File name:
WALLBLK1

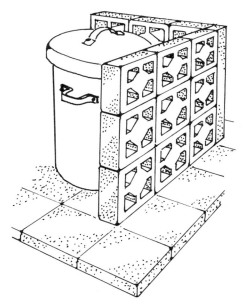

Design a garden walling block

The blocks are cast from concrete. They each measure 300 × 300 × 150 mm. The open spaces in each block are there to reduce weight and allow some light to come through the wall.

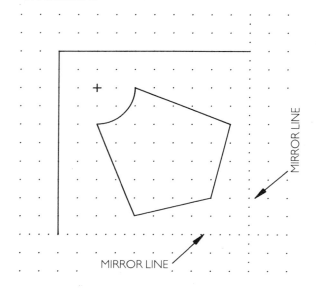

MIRROR LINE

MIRROR LINE

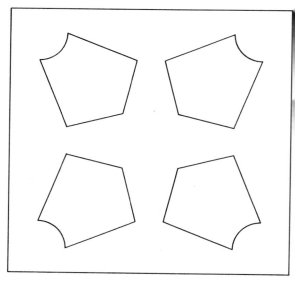

insertion point

Drawn on *Bitstik*

An isometric drawing of your design can give a more realistic view of what the wall will look like. Set an isometric grid. If you are working on *Bitstik*, place the drawing at the screen centre. This will give a point to use for location. Use the same bottom corner for insertion on other software. File the block. In this example the left-hand wall was drawn and filed. The drawing was brought out of file and mirrored for the right-hand wall. Finally, the centre pier was added.

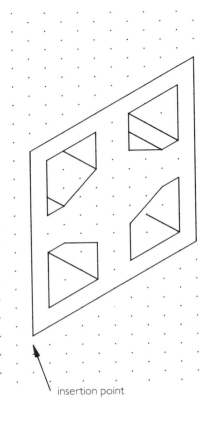

insertion point

This pattern is produced by using a unit of four blocks. A single pattern can be mirrored to produce the orthographic view. You will find that a left-hand and a right-hand block are needed for this isometric view.

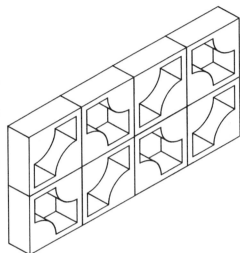

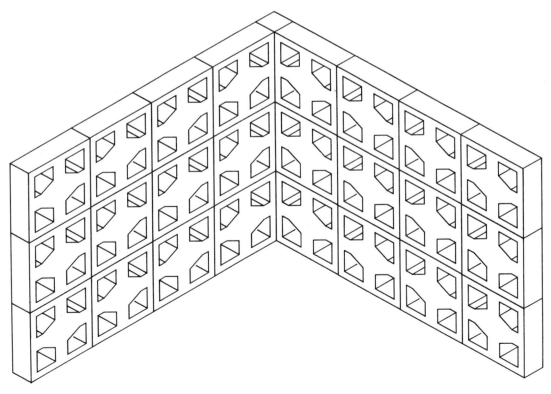

Drawn on *Bitstik*

26
PORTABLE RADIO CASE

The tuning scale should be drawn first and filed.
Knob designs may already be on file.
Other features need not be filed; they will vary
with each design.

When your plot is complete, colour the designs
with crayon or felt tip pens.

File name:
TUNESCLE

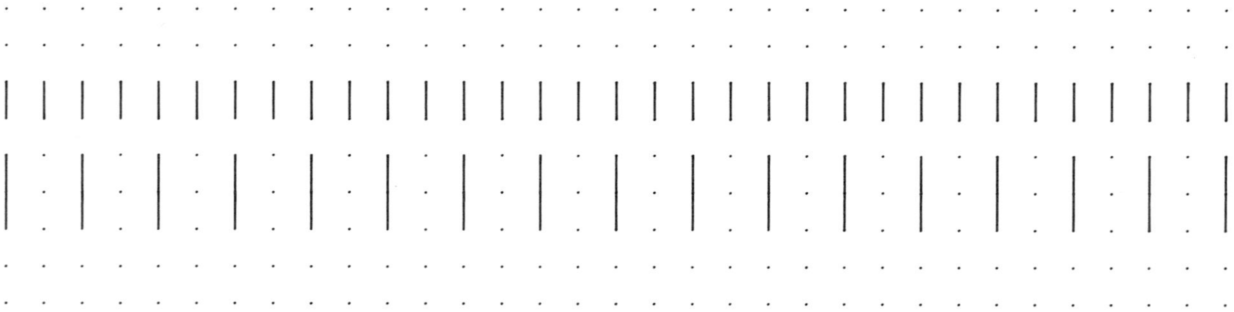

Design a case for a portable radio

Make a series of preliminary sketches on squared
paper, considering all of the features which a
portable radio would need.
- Tuning scale
- Cursor control knob
- Battery storage
- On/Off/Volume control knob or knobs or sliders
- The shape of the case
- How the case is to be carried
- Holes in the case for sound
- Plug for earphones (think of the best place for
this)
Material: Moulded plastic

File name:
PORTRAD1

TUNSCLE

KNOB 1   with circle added

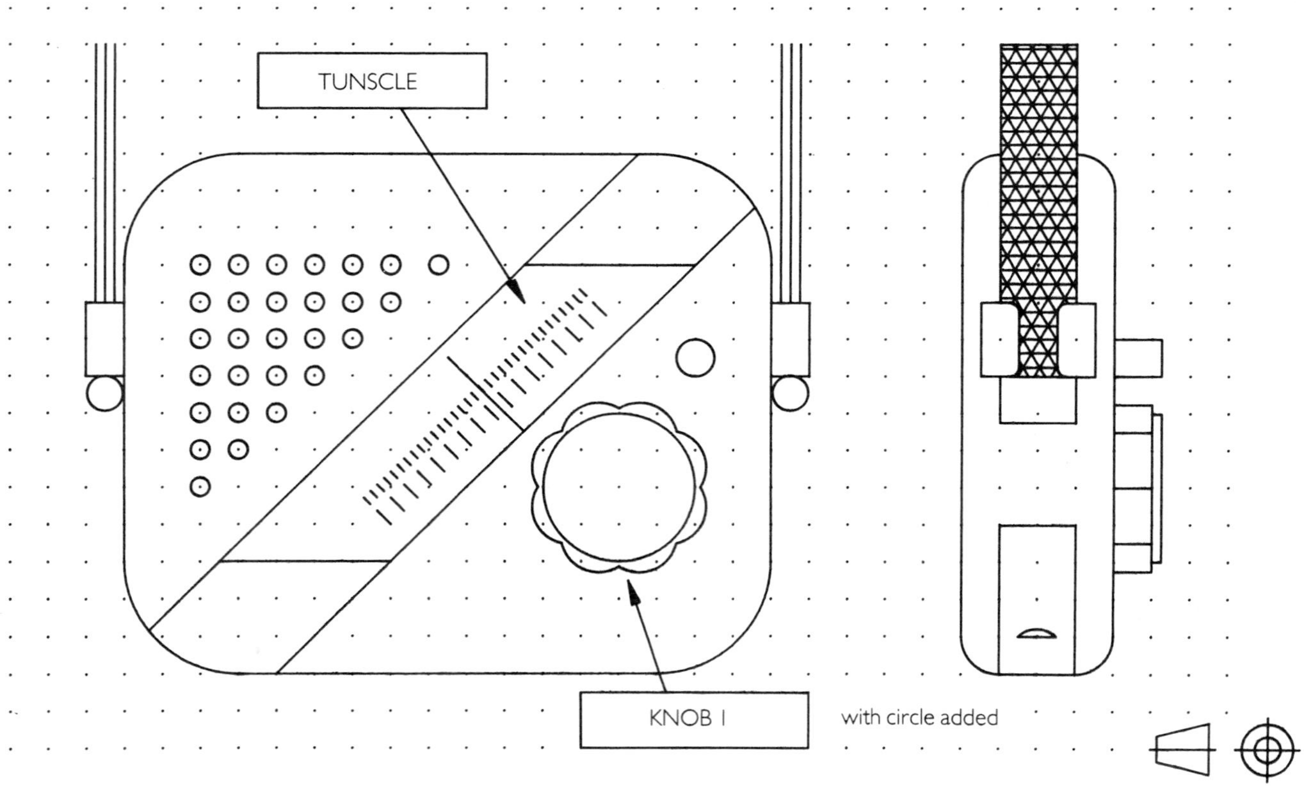

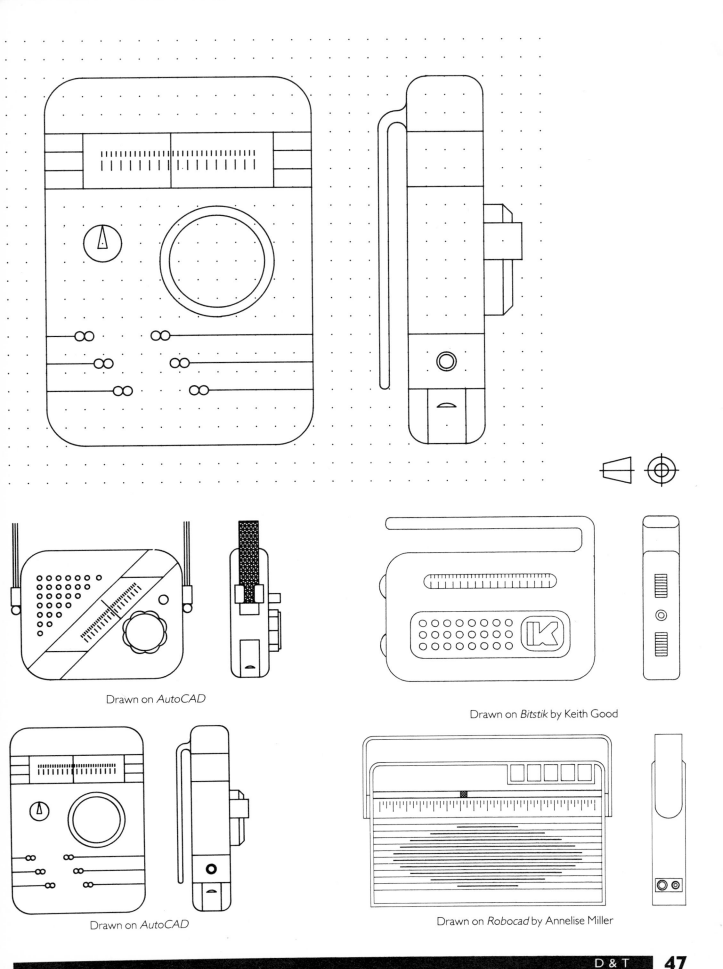

Drawn on *AutoCAD*

Drawn on *Bitstik* by Keith Good

Drawn on *AutoCAD*

Drawn on *Robocad* by Annelise Miller

27
DESIGN A GARDEN

Gardens can be designed to suit the needs of many different people. A garden used by a retired couple will have to meet different needs from a garden used by children. Plan views of some of the things commonly found in a garden are given; you may wish to re-design them.

File name:
SHRUB
(Use for small trees and plants)

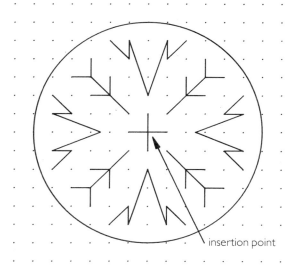

insertion point

File name: SHED (Roof may be left plain)

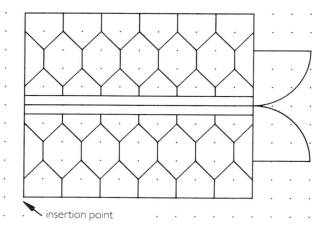

insertion point

File name: POND

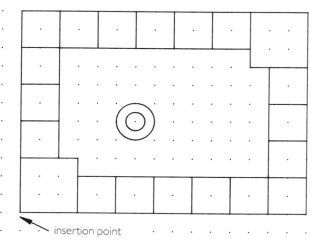

insertion point

File name:
SEAT

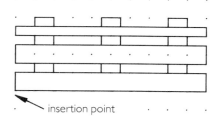

insertion point

File name:
SWING

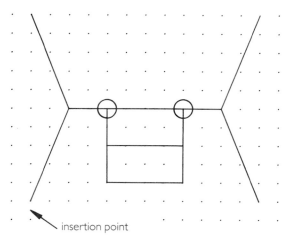

insertion point

File name: GREENHOUSE (GREENHSE)

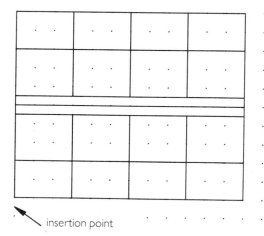

insertion point

How to organise your work

1 Decide upon a size and shape of plot. For example, this could be your own garden.
2 Decide who will use the garden. Write out a simple brief and a list of the things to be included in the design. Ideas can be found in gardening books. *The Small Garden* by John Brookes (Aura Books) is very suitable for this purpose.

Remember, irregular shapes use a lot of memory. Try to design using lines, arcs and circles. These parts are worth filing in the library if they are to be repeated or moved about in the course of your designing.

3 Draw a plan of the garden showing a portion of the house with windows and doors. Take into account views from windows and the need to provide paths and a paved area.
4 Make freehand pictorial views of the results.

Garden for a retired couple

Garden for children

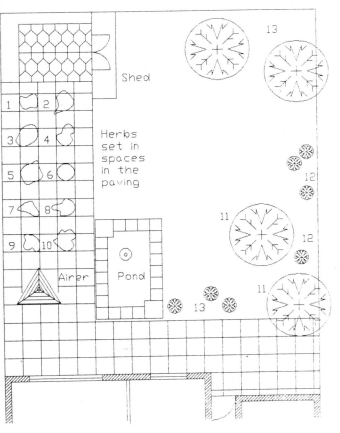

Drawn on *AUTOSKETCH*, printed on a dot matrix printer

28
ALPHABET DESIGN

Design an alphabet of letters which will be suitable for use on computer screens and which is capable of being drawn on CAD software. This will mean limiting the shapes to those which can be drawn using lines and arcs. Make sketches of the letters on squared paper. The special features of your design must be capable of being repeated on every letter. Plan the important heights above and below a centre line. Draw each letter on the screen separately and file away. On *Bitstik*, use the centre of the screen as the insertion point by working to the right of the screen.

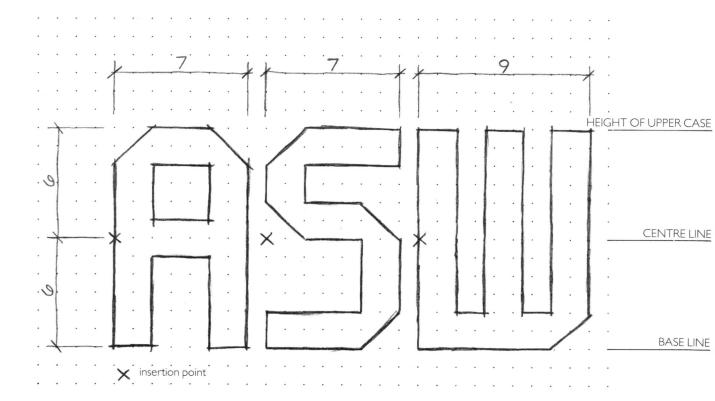

× insertion point

Using the letters

Mark out lines for each row of letters.

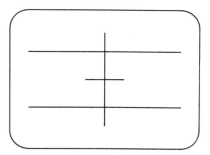

Use the grid and insertion point for accurate placing of the letters.

Turn off the grid. Look at the spaces between letters for any large gaps. Use MOVE and correct the spacing by eye to improve it. Erase the guide lines.

CRAFT DESIGN
AND
TECHNOLOGY

Changing proportions

The first version of 'school' (top left in the rectangle), is printed at the original proportions as designed and filed. The other two have been altered by changing the X or Y scale factor. In this way, you can make letters fit into a particular size or area. For example, the words 'school' are all the same length, but they have been manipulated in scale and height to fit together into a rectangle.

City alphabet

SCHOOL SCHOOL
SCHOOL SCHOOL

Fill in and mirror

Try using a filled letter or figure and mirror it to make interesting patterns. Use this method sparingly: filling in uses a lot of memory.

The 'quick brown fox' sentence is good to use in examples because it contains all of the letters of the alphabet and it shows how the alphabet will look when it is being read.

ABCDEFGH
IJKLMNOP
QRSTUVWX
YZ

TIM   PAUL

Paul Gibbinson and Tim Harding

THE QUICK
BROWN
FOX
JUMPS
OVER THE
LAZY DOG

John Worsley

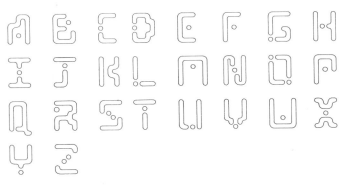

THE QUICK BROWN
FOX JUMPS OVER
THE LAZY DOG

Jean Lytollis

29 DESIGNING SYMBOLS & ICONS

These are designs which could be used for trade symbols. Work out a set of designs to cover the subjects on your timetable.

A symbol is a drawing which represents an object, idea or process. A good symbol should 'trigger' an instant recognition of what it stands for. This is why symbols, or **icons**, are so useful on software menus. When designing symbols you should make a list of special qualities about the subject and develop them into visual features by simplifying detail and exaggerating the features. Keep to the grid, or half grid. Reduce the design to lines, circles or arcs.

Symbol for a dressmaker   Cotton reels, buttons, fabric patterns

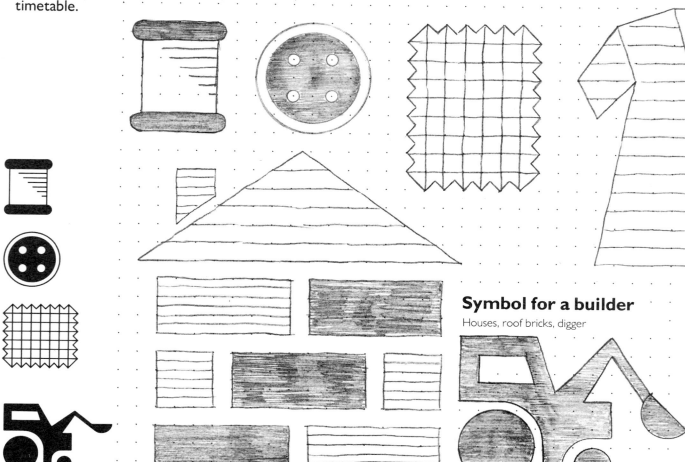

Symbol for a builder
Houses, roof bricks, digger

Symbol for a jeweller   Silverware, facets, diamonds

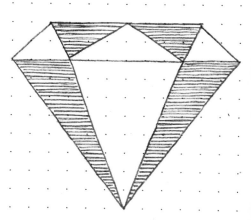

30
SYMBOLS FOR A
DIY BOOK

A publisher is producing a 'do it yourself' book about simply-constructed furniture. Each job in the book will have a cutting and tool list. Instead of using a written statement about the tools needed for each job it is intended to show a set of symbols. Design a suitable set of symbols bearing in mind the need to reduce them to the size of the holiday brochure symbols shown alongside.

Tools
Pencil, rule, try square, tenon saw, hand drill, 4 mm and 6 mm drill bits, screwdriver, hammer, mitreblock, awl, glasspaper.

Symbols
To fit a 12 mm square.

Holiday brochure symbols – finished size

 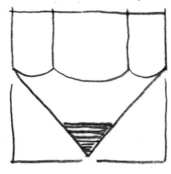 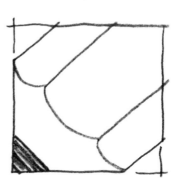

 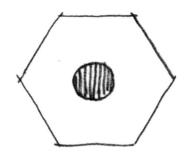 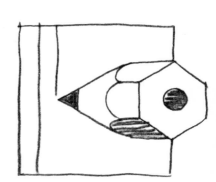

Out of the six preliminary ideas two have been drawn and plotted.

Note how a symbol which is successful in a large format may lose clarity when it is reduced to a very small format.

What do you think about the cut-away at the bottom of the square? The idea is to emphasise the pencil point. Is it successful? Can the same device be used on the other symbols?

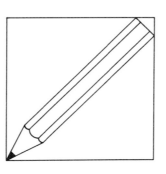 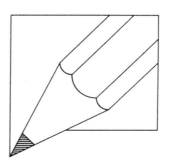

31
DESIGNING A LOGO

Ideas for a logo designed for a firm of estate agents with initials AS. Designed by Ashley Stockwell.

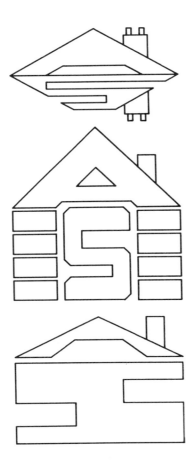

How a compression can improve visual appearance

Keep the X scale at 0, and reduce the Y scale. Try various reductions.

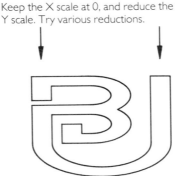

A logogram, usually shortened to logo, is a device of words or letters incorporated in a symbolic design used to identify a firm or organisation. The estate agent logo illustrates this definition. You can see that the letters all form parts of a house: letters in a symbolic design. Logos play an important part in identifying the makers of household and industrial products of all kinds. They now serve the same purpose on television and electronic information devices of all kinds.

Design a logo for a school, a department, a club, a business, a TV series or a software package. The finished logo should be plotted in three sizes which will be useful for different purposes. The smallest size should be suitable for use on a letterhead or business card.

Some design considerations

Is a full title necessary or just letters?
Can library letters be used? The Friendship Club letters are from a *Robocom* City Alphabet disc. If you have an alphabet from a previous exercise it may be suitable.
Can shapes be incorporated which have symbolic meaning?

How to organise your work

1 Sketch on grid paper your ideas, shapes and symbols

2 Split your design into separate parts – letters and shapes – and file in different compartments.
Use the computer facilities to manipulate the parts until you obtain a satisfactory design. Stretch or compress the letters or shapes. Look for an improvement in proportions and balance. Try a variety of combinations from the same basic drawings. Look to see whether the detail is lost when reducing the logo to the smallest required size.

Points for you to consider about the design

● Is the upper part of the B top heavy?
● Is the smallest size logo still clear and readable?
● Would it look better completely filled in?

Here are the stages in designing a logo for a club called the *Friendship Club*. The same handshake could be the graphic title shot for a video. Think of a programme title to add as an alternative assignment.

The handshake has been selected as a symbol of friendship. The original drawing would use a lot of computer memory so it has been converted into straight lines. On *Bitstik* software, MOVE only operates on parts which have been filed. Therefore, the different parts of the design should be drawn on the screen and filed separately.

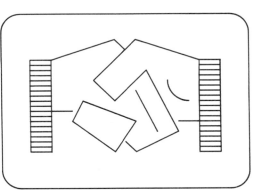

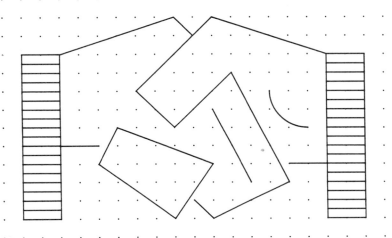

Move the parts about the screen into a variety of different positions. Draw as many different designs as possible. Judge the results and, finally, select one design as your *Friendship Club* logo.

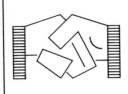

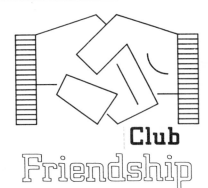

32
DESIGNING GRAPHS & HISTOGRAMS

When more than one graph is involved, comparison can be made easier by placing one graph on top of the other. However, where lines cross look for ambiguities. How many different ways could the lines go on the graphs shown below?

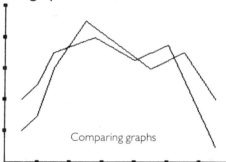

Comparing graphs

To make the situation clear, use a different linetype such as dotted or chain and label each line.

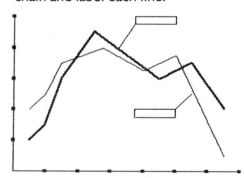

Manipulating the impression given by a graph

Graphs are frequently used to present an instant impression of situations in such areas as finance and politics. Look at these two graphs. They represent the same situation. What impression is given by each graph when read separately?

Graphs are used to compare change. The rate of change is generally easier to understand if it is given visually rather than numerically. Look at the three examples shown below. They all take the same figures and display them in different ways. Which method do you think is the most effective way of showing rate of change? What differences can you see between graphs and histograms?

Graphs and histograms show changes in quantity visually

TABLE

X	1	2	3	4	5
Y	2	1	4	2	1

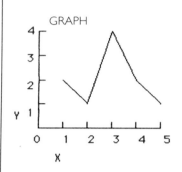

GRAPH

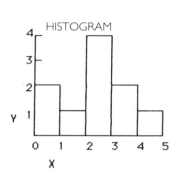

HISTOGRAM

The same design principles could be applied to histograms. In this example the white histogram is not covered by any of the chequered histogram. What would you do if the chequered second column was 3 spaces high?

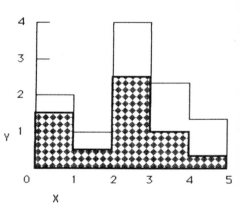

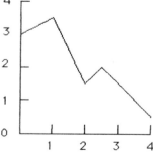

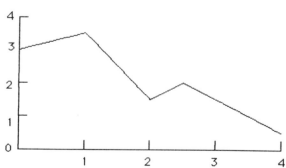

The first graph shows a strong downward slope. By stretching the horizontal scale a less dramatic impression is created. In what context would such a graph be seen? Should graphics be used in this way?

Graphs without proper origins

In a similar way, showing only part of a graph can give a misleading impression. The first version shows a very dramatic situation with the line heading off the bottom of the graph. In reality, if the lower portion of the graph down to zero is shown, a very different impression is given.

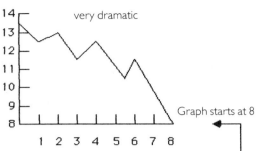

very dramatic

Graph starts at 8

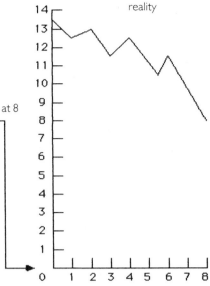

reality

This is how the graph should be drawn. It puts the fall into a proper context. However, drawing the graph this way takes up a lot of room. Therefore, these are some of the techniques which can be used in order to present a more truthful impression.

Graphs drawn on MacDraw

When space is limited

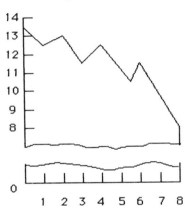

- Use a break technique or 'convention'.

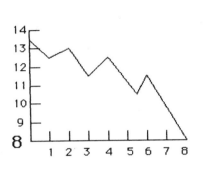

- Use a large numeral to emphasise that the X axis does not start at zero.

Holiday weather

These figures show a comparison between the weather in the Balearic Islands and London during the winter period.

Make an attractive graphic presentation for use on a television programme, or in a holiday brochure. Incorporate symbols for temperature and sunshine in the design.

Average hours of sunshine

	OCT	NOV	DEC	JAN	FEB	MAR	APR
Balearics	6	5	5	5	6	6	7
London	3	2	1	2	2	4	6

Average temperature (°F)

	OCT	NOV	DEC	JAN	FEB	MAR	APR
Balearics	73	64	59	57	59	63	66
London	57	50	44	43	44	50	55

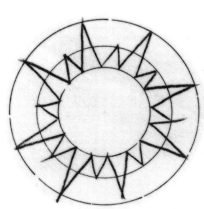

33 DESIGNING BAR DIAGRAMS

Some business software packages will allow you to draw graphs and other statistical diagrams simply by feeding in figures. However, they are designed to deal with very specific cases. Numerical quantities are not easy for most people to grasp. Your task as a designer is to take these quantities and display them so that they are more readily understood.

Quantities which are spread about are difficult to count quickly.

For example:
Which is greater, X or Y?

X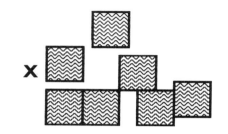

Y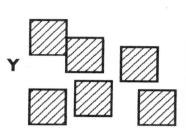

The task is made easier by arranging the squares in rows. Then the difference is easily seen by comparing the lengths.

X

Y

Statistics shown in this way are called **Bar Diagrams**.

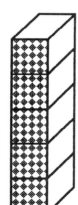

They can be drawn horizontally, upright or made into three-dimensional diagrams.

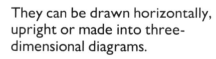

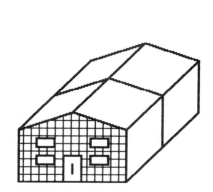

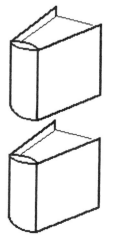

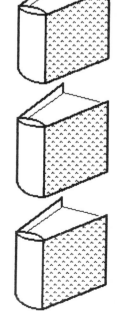

Pictographs

Symbols are used to represent the subject matter.

Each symbol is assigned a given quantity

 = 100

For larger amounts use more symbols

250

A visual comparison can be made by organising the material as a bar diagram.

**HOUSES BUILT IN NEWTOWN
1988-1989
Each house = 100**

1988

1989

This type of visual comparison is not recommended. Although a difference is clearly seen, the precise difference is not easy to calculate.

It is difficult to compare area; much easier to compare length.

Make a visual comparison between the area and population of these Commonwealth countries.

The list can be increased by taking more statistics from *The Commonwealth Factbook* (Commonwealth Secretariat, 1987).

	Area in km²	Population in millions
Australia	8 million	16
Britain	1 million	57
Canada	10 million	26
	All figures have been rounded up	

34
WEATHER CHARTS

Television symbols

The symbols for BBC Television Weather Forecasts are shown below, each with a short explanation. The symbols form a basic language of weather types which can be extended by using various combinations.

This assignment will show you the use of the computer for designing weather charts. Once symbols and maps are on file, making a chart is not the laborious task it once was and updating is fairly easy. These are the approximate proportions for the BBC weather symbols. The assignment is based on them. As an alternative assignment, re-design the symbols.

You can produce the sunshine symbol by various methods, depending on the type of software being used. It could be mirrored from the quarter shown, or it could be arrayed from a single mark. File away as single symbols.

 TEMPERATURE: Red figures on a yellow background give positive temperature in degrees centigrade. Black figures on a light blue background give freezing temperatures, i.e. below zero centigrade.

 SUNSHINE: The yellow symbol represents the sun; the red figures in the centre show a temperature of 25 degrees centigrade.

 CLOUD: A white cloud symbol indicates fine-weather clouds that may be relatively thin and patchy.

 A black cloud represents the thicker and more widespread clouds often associated with dull weather.

 SUNNY INTERVALS: The sun symbol used in conjunction with a cloud in this way means some sunshine as well, particularly if the white cloud symbol is used.

 RAIN: The dark blue tear-drop symbols beneath the cloud indicate rain.

 RAIN SHOWERS AND SUNNY INTERVALS: A combination of rain, cloud and sun represents sunny intervals and rain showers.

 SNOW: The white symbols beneath the cloud indicate snow.

 SLEET: The rain and snow symbols together beneath the cloud indicate sleet.

 THUNDERSTORM: The symbol of a black cloud with a yellow flash represents the possibility of thunder and lightning.

WIND SPEED & DIRECTION: The black symbol represents the wind speed and direction, the speed printed in the centre in white is in miles per hour.

F O G FOG: Fog is not represented by a specific symbol; it is indicated by words on the map in the general areas likely to be affected.

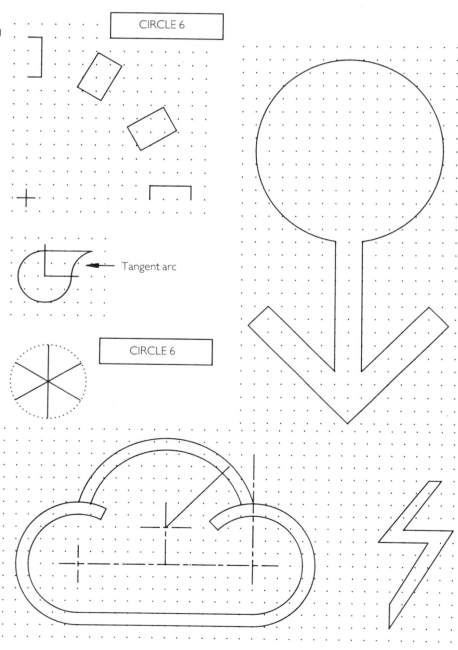

CIRCLE 6

Tangent arc

CIRCLE 6

Draw a weather chart of England, Wales and Scotland, using the following information. Use a map from the file. Either MAPEWS or MAPEWS3D

- - - - - - - - - - - - - - - -

• Below a line from the Bristol Channel to the Wash.

Sunshine.
Maximum temperature 25°.

- - - - - - - - - - - - - - - -

• Below a line from the Firth of Clyde to the Firth of Forth.

Rain showers and sunny intervals.
Maximum temperature 22°.

- - - - - - - - - - - - - - - -

• Above the top area

Rain.
Maximum temperature 15°.

Windspeed in all areas 35 mph from the south-west.

- - - - - - - - - - - - - - - -

Extra assignment

• Instead of the above information use up-to-date reports from a local meteorological office.

Drawn on *AutoCAD*

Develop this idea for a graphic display of local weather. It should show daily temperature as well as giving some indication of the main weather of each day.

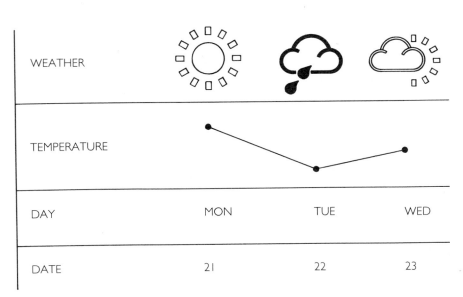

35
ADVERTISING

For best results when designing an advert, use a **paint** type of software which will allow a freer treatment than the usual CAD software. Paint programmes are easier to use for freehand drawing although grids are also available for use on the menu. They also give a variety of type fonts and a wide choice of fill-in textures.

LANDSCAPE GARDENING

John Smith ,
25, Railway Villas,
Hollerton.

LANDSCAPE GARDENING

John Smith ,
25, Railway Villas,
Hollerton.

Electronic composing gives you the freedom to move and change things easily until satisfied with the design. For example, the balance of the landscape gardening design could be improved by moving the trees to the right.

DISCO Admission FREE

Friday   20 September
6 pm in the School Hall

BLUEBERRY FARM
Pick - Your - Own

	JUNE	JULY	AUGUST	SEPT
Strawberries				
Raspberries				
Redcurrants				
Blackcurrants				
Runner beans				
Sweet corn				

Open daily 10 a.m. - 6 p.m.

Numerous assignments can be found. For example, tickets, business cards, small posters for the school play, disco or sports day, and so on.

Drawn on MacPaint

36

COLLECTING BOX

name:
OLLBOX

This is a collecting box made from thin cardboard. It has been designed so that it can be sent through the post and easily assembled without glue. Draw and plot it on thin card. Score all lines before folding and make up a plain box. The triangular pieces at the corners of the box fold inside. Score the corner centre line on the other side of the card. Hook the small bottom flaps together first, then the large bottom flaps.

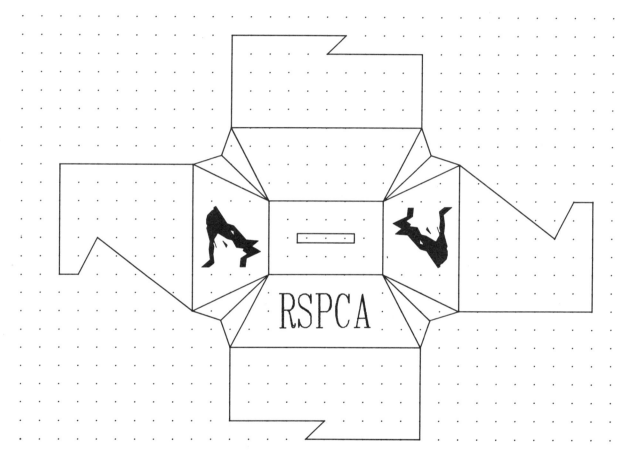

After this task of folding up the box, recall the drawing to the screen and devise a simple way of showing how the flaps are folded. You can use text, numbers or diagrams.

Choose a charity such as the Royal Society for the Prevention of Cruelty to Animals (RSPCA) and place the initials or a logo so that they will be seen when the box is standing on a shelf. Colour it in with pens or paint.

37
PETS SYMBOL

Draw a grid over the
orginal drawing.

Existing drawings or symbols can be transferred to
the screen by using this simple technique. Draw a
grid over the original drawing and use the crossing
points for reference in converting the outline into
a series of lines. The original symbol, shown below
with the grid drawn on it, is taken from *Instant
Symbols and Graphics*, published by Graphics
World (a book of copyright free artwork).

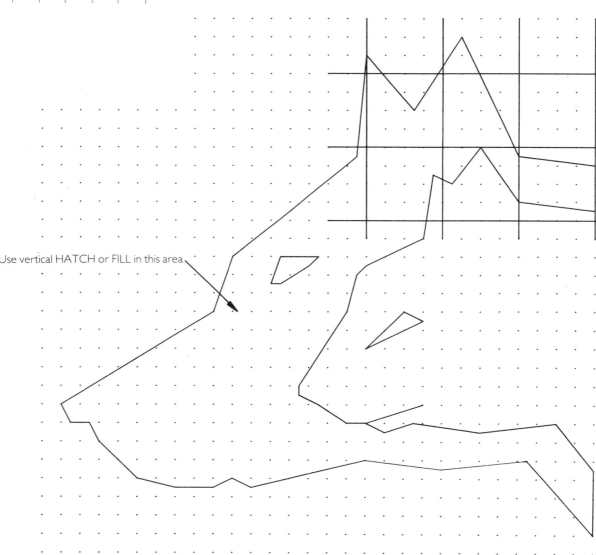

Use vertical HATCH or FILL in this area